Creating a ***Winning*** Game Plan

~ *For Janice* ~

Creating a Winning Game Plan

The Secondary Teacher's Playbook

Michael D. Gose

CORWIN PRESS, INC.
A Sage Publications Company
Thousand Oaks, California

Copyright © 1999 by Corwin Press, Inc.

All rights reserved. No part of this book may be reproduced or utilized in any form or by any means, electronic or mechanical, including photocopying, recording, or by any information storage and retrieval system, without permission in writing from the publisher.

For information address:

Corwin Press, Inc.
A Sage Publications Company
2455 Teller Road
Thousand Oaks, California 91320
E-mail: order@corwinpress.com

SAGE Publications Ltd.
6 Bonhill Street
London EC2A 4PU
United Kingdom

SAGE Publications India Pvt. Ltd.
M-32 Market
Greater Kailash I
New Delhi 110 048 India

Library of Congress Cataloging-in-Publication Data

Gose, Michael D. (Michael Douglas)
  Creating a winning game plan: The secondary teacher's playbook by Michael D. Gose.
    p. cm.
    ISBN 0-8039-6790-X (cloth: acid-free paper)
    ISBN 0-8039-6791-8 (pbk.: acid-free paper)
    1. High school teaching. 2. Effective teaching. 3. Education, Secondary—Curricula. I. Title.
    LB1737.A3G67 2999
    373.1102—dc21   98-40272

This book is printed on acid-free paper.

99 00 01 02 03 04 05   7 6 5 4 3 2 1

Editorial Assistant: Julia Parnell
Production Editor: Denise Santoyo
Production Assistant: Patricia Zeman
Typesetter/Designer: Janelle LeMaster
Cover Designer: Tracy E. Miller

Contents

Preface	vii
Purpose	vii
Description of Contents	viii
The Book as a Game Plan	ix
Limits of the Book	x
Survival and Success	xi
Finally	xii
Acknowledgments	xiii
About the Author	xiv
1. Creating the Game Plan	**1**
Introducing the Game Plan	1
Putting on Your Game Face	5
Contextualizing Your Game Plan	12
The Pep Talk	17
Miscellaneous Tips on Establishing Yourself	21
2. Planning Lessons and Teaching Strategies	**26**
What to Teach: The Basic Outline of Subjects	26
Using the Range of Teaching Strategies and Media	41

Organization and Pacing the Curriculum	55
Grading, Evaluation, and Assessment	67
Motivating Students	86
Miscellaneous Tips on Teaching	91
Teaching the Hidden Curriculum	95

3. Managing Classroom Behavior — **102**

Expectations and Procedures	104
Mike Myers' Six Rules for More Savvy Teaching	116
So Now What Do I Do? Physical Ploys to Affect Student Behavior	117
20 Classic Teaching Mistakes	123
Classroom Games and How to Play Them	131
A Fourth Grade Dilemma, A Trick of the Trade	136
Comments on the Philosophy of Discipline	137
Reading Levels and Discipline Problems	141
Miscellaneous Tips on Classroom Management	143

4. Thriving in Teaching — **149**

The Emergency Plan	149
Thriving as a Teacher	151
Resource A. Almost Instant Lesson Plans for Most Subjects	157
Resource B. Sample A, B, and C Activities	172
Resource C. A Scavenger Hunt to Encourage Resourcefulness	193
Resource D. Homework Assignments	194
Resource E. Annotated Resources	196

References — 201

Preface

Purpose

I wrote this book over a 20-year period of time. I was formerly both an elementary school teacher and a high school English teacher. Later, as a high school vice principal and principal, I was responsible for faculty evaluation and development. Then, as a college director of secondary education, I was responsible for the curriculum and methods course and the supervision of student teachers. Most of the writing for this book was simply my response to what my student teachers and beginning teachers needed for their own classrooms. (I am hopeful that experienced teachers also will read this book with some delight and amusement, and perhaps find some additions to their repertoire of skills.)

Indeed, my own experience as a beginning teacher suggested that such a book could be career saving. I so well remember my own feelings as a beginning teacher: anxiety bordering on panic. Not so much on my first day of teaching. More toward the end of the first week, when I realized that none of my summer plans, none of my assigned textbooks, none of my supplementary materials were going to work with my particular classes, my students. What had gone wrong?

Two truths:

1. Teacher preparation programs are all underappreciated.
2. No teacher preparation program can ever fully prepare someone for the realities of teaching.

I felt overwhelmed. There were a billion things to know. I needed one idea that would work tomorrow. If I could just get through tomorrow with some success, I could worry about the day after tomorrow later.

The wealth of knowledge that I had been taught on teaching only made me feel guilty and overly incompetent. Reader, do not misunderstand. From all external reviews, I had success even as a beginning teacher. And, then and now, I felt the study of Bloom, Erikson, Tyler, Eisner, et al. was invaluable. But, the scholarship on education did not become truly meaningful until I was able to get through each of my own class periods with some level of success.

The only three books that I found at the beginning of my career that provided me with immediate help were two by Jenny Gray: *A Teacher's Survival Guide* and *Teaching Without Tears* (1968; 1969—both long out of print) and Jim Herndon's (1971) *How to Survive in Your Native Land*. Three decades later, I intend for this book to have that same savviness that will be immediately helpful. This book is written to help you attain an entry level of success on which to build all the remaining years of your career.

~ Description of Contents

The book is divided into four chapters and a Resources section. The organization is logical in that it moves from context to teaching to discipline to thriving in teaching. Certainly, you can read the book from cover to cover, but as a playbook, you can also read it out of sequence according to interest and need. Chapter 1 introduces the idea of the game plan. The presumption is that there are underlying strategies for classroom success and successful play makes for more enjoyable teaching. This is a book about enjoying the necessary contest between teachers and students. It is about creating a winning game plan for success with students. It is never meant to be about winning at a student's expense.

Chapter 2 is where most books on teaching start: curriculum and instruction. This chapter is organized around the four questions of the Tyler (1950) rationale: (1) What should we teach? (2) What teaching techniques should we use? (3) How should we organize that teaching? (4) How should we evaluate our results? Ralph Tyler said in retrospect that he would have added (5) How do we motivate students to do this academic work?

To be great is to be misunderstood.

Chapter 3 emphasizes classroom management and discipline. It highlights minimizing discipline problems by running an effective curriculum and having sound policies and procedures. It also recognizes the inevitability of some problems, and discusses rules, mistakes, games, tips, and a brief review of four particular approaches to discipline, and then ends with an explanation of how students' poor reading skills are often accompanied by discipline problems.

Chapter 4 contains an emergency plan and an emergency card, reducing the principles of this game plan approach to its most manageable form. This chapter then discusses moving from the survival mode to the success mode and thriving in teaching.

The Resources provide prototypical lesson plan formats, sample lesson plans for each part of the class period, a section on homework, and lists of recommended readings, films, and Web sites.

The Book as a Game Plan

This book is a game plan in that it emphasizes having a sense of gamesmanship and it has plans for each of the major areas of teaching in terms of methods and classroom management. The book is a playbook in that there are recommended ploys, strategies, feints, moves, and tactics for teaching and disciplining effectively. The words *game* and *play* are favorites because I am convinced teaching should be an enjoyable profession, certainly a serious undertaking, but also a lot of fun.

Creating a Winning Game Plan: The Secondary Teacher's Playbook is only a title, however. It is not meant to be an overextended metaphor. Areas of the book such as what to teach and expectations and procedures are straightforward. Those areas are more like the rules of play that would be included in a playbook. It is more in the areas of implementation of your plans that I look for the humor, the gamesmanship, the fun.

An alternate metaphor, or at least analogy, for how I envision this book is that of a toolbox. A toolbox does not suggest the gamesmanship and enjoyment that a playbook does, but I do see each separate part of this book as being akin to individual tools. Naturally, there are major tools, such as the outline of basic subjects and expectations and procedures. There are also small, idiosyncratic tools, such as the fourth grade dilemma and the miscellaneous tips that end each of the first three chapters. Thus, these are intended to be tools for creating, repairing, and tweaking all the discernible components of teaching.

The tools are organized in a fashion that should help you find them. But as I said before, the book does not demand to be read sequentially. To change metaphors once more, the book is a collection, a storehouse, a kit, a handbook, a toolbox, a playbook of the most immediately useful materials to run your own classroom.

~ Limits of the Book

This is not an "all you need to know about teaching" book. This book is intended to help you get off to a good start as a classroom teacher. This is a specific focus. The suggestions depend on you being able to take advantage of your own formal education to make good decisions about what is worthwhile to teach in your classroom. Although the emphasis is on method, technique, and strategy, none of this will compensate for shallow or hollow curricular content. Your students are likely to spend far more time watching television than they spend in the classroom. Do not waste any of that precious classroom time.

What about educational research? Educational theory? History of schooling? First, you will most probably have taken foundation courses in education in a credential program that set a context for any discussion of teaching methods. Second, I am convinced that one must have teaching experience before one can truly appreciate the professional literature. Until you have your own questions, your answers are not likely to be fully meaningful.

Until I found out what worked and didn't work for me personally in the classroom, what the limitations were beyond my own lack of experience and skill, I could not have had the deep appreciation of educational historian David Tyack (1974) showing me how schools got the way they are; educational philosopher John Dewey (1938) validating the emphasis so many teachers have on activities and educational experience; educational connoisseur Elliot Eisner (1991) clarifying a metaphor for all my teaching, the enlightened eye; educator Paulo Freire (1970) establishing the roles of teacher-learner and learner-teacher; or educational psychologist Nate Gage (Gage & Berliner, 1979) reviewing the best of the best research on both the theory and the practice of teaching. Such perspectives are profoundly important. I would make such works required reading, reading to be done before you start teaching and again after you start teaching. This book hopes to be immediately helpful; it in no way substitutes for the necessary fullness of the ongoing search for what it means to be a teacher.

Survival and Success

Will this game plan work for everyone? No. The beginning teacher who does not have the will to be in charge of the classroom is doomed. The person who cannot accept the inherent job conditions (i.e., 36 people working in a relatively small room) will not stay in the profession. The person who is not student-centered will never truly enjoy the work. But for those who realize the great joy of the give and take of the classroom, this book has the prospect of being both enjoyable and heuristic.

I have called this book a "playbook" because it is my game plan. I presume that any teacher who reads this book will derive his or her own game plan. I fervently believe that this book has the prospect of helping you become a better teacher and most probably will help you enjoy teaching more. I think this book can help you *survive* so that you can *succeed*. The book reflects a view of teaching that often shows up in the trenches (to change metaphors), but seldom shows up in books or professional journals. This approach has the prospect of making you much more savvy about the realities and complexities of teaching.

This book wants to share with you the gamesmanship that makes for enjoyable teaching.

~ Finally

I like to point out to my own students that Emerson (1967) said that to be great is to be misunderstood. I delight when a student points out to me that that is not the same thing as saying to be misunderstood is to be great. That's the type of playful give-and-take that works very well for me and with me. The longer I worked on this book, the more I realized that it is written for the prospective teacher or teacher who will recognize and laugh at my pretensions, hyperbole, and tendency to amuse myself in print. I do not apologize for the chattiness of this book. I want to emphasize that it is my game plan, my point of view. I distrust writing that tries too hard to be objective. I tend to make my strongest recommendations as advice and my more idiosyncratic practices as personal anecdotes. My belief is that the more I reveal about my own biases, the more you can take the recommendations with a grain of salt, react to them, and make your own plans accordingly. Recently, an acquaintance of mine arrived at the same hotel where I had stayed in London. I recommended a number of restaurants in the area. When she left a couple of weeks later, she hadn't been to any of those restaurants, but she was willing to share her own recommendations with me. I like that.

I hope that you will find this book useful. I hope you will recognize its intended playfulness. I trust you will forgive the seemingly chatty and overly personal quality because it is my way of suggesting the way I personalize my own teaching, and how I would want you to personalize teaching in your own way. In fact, I was reluctant to write a book for an audience larger than my own classes, so to take this risk, I felt I must try to stay consistent with how I write and teach for my own students, the students who know me personally. I have written imagining myself as a coach and the readers as members of my team. To date, all my student teachers have been surprisingly savvy for beginning teachers, but each has his or her own unique way of being successful in the classroom. In a sense, no student ever has the teacher he or she deserves. My book is only a place to start. I believe that if you look at the underlying assumptions of this book, you will see that I have encouraged you to be student-oriented in your leadership role, to find enjoyment in your teaching, and to commit to career-long learning as a teacher.

Acknowledgments

I would like to express my thanks and appreciation to my editor, Alice Foster, for her belief in this book and to Robert Escudero for his great help in the preparation of the manuscript. I would also like to thank my great friend, Darryl Shimazu, for his drawings. For almost 30 years now, he has had the uncanny ability to draw what's in my mind, only better. I would like to acknowledge and thank *California English* for its permission to reuse my article, "Making Small Groups Work"; Edmund T. Ember, Carolyn M. Evertson, Barbara S. Clements, Julie P. Sanford, and Murray E. Worsham for permission to use their list of expectations and procedures from *Organizing and Managing the Junior High Classroom* (1981); *The High School Journal* for permission to reuse my article, "Classroom Games and How to Play Them"; *Learning Magazine,* for permission to reuse my idea, a new-old pattern for classroom interaction; *Instructor,* where some of my common faults in teaching and miscellaneous tips have appeared; and the College Board, for its permission to use its outline of basic academic subjects (1983). I was unable to locate Mike Myers, to whom I credit the six rules for more savvy teaching. I hope that my recollection of his presentation at the California Council of Teachers does his ideas justice.

I would particularly like to acknowledge the following former students who had influence on the creation of this material: Mona Oxford, Bev Bolton Mitcham, Sue Constuble Briquelet, Peggy Boyd, Judy Brown Square, Robert Escudero, Frank Cruz, Chris Grimm, Lisa Kodama, Kris Klinger, Jennifer Wolford, Mary Haws, Pat Iseke, Marian Moyher, Audrea Walker, Cathy Bellini, David Poole, Linda Graham, John Flaherty, Fides Orpilla, Carolyn Wilson, Russell Lee-Sung, Tim McMannon, Kimberly Bottomley, Robin Drake, Michael Walker, Darlynn Wilhelm, Charlie Park, Scott Carlson, Caroline Bennett Dewey, Tanja Carter, Monica Wagener Duran, Ty Delong, Brett Landis, Charee Scharf Landis, Greg Scott, Tony Fuller, Tiffany Laster Biggs, Cynthia Jones Wade, AnneMarie Perez, Damian Corbin Jenkins, Bill Crockett, Helen Gomez, Susan Kim, James Moshier, Suzanne Yates, Michi Oluk, Ken Montgomery, Jennifer Nelson Moshier, Rob Sayles, Suzanna Shenk, Randall Walters, Wendy Willis, Brandon Blevins, Brian Crum, Tricia Lindquist, Cherilyn Redwine, Amy Repp, David Soberg, Monica Sousa, April Judd, Selina Pabon, Eric Brubaker, Laura Gerard, Michael Harris, Alison Olver, Drew Passalacqua, and Whitney Shelburne.

About the Author

Michael D. Gose is Professor of Teacher Education at Pepperdine University in Malibu, California. He has a bachelor's degree from Occidental College, masters' degrees from Stanford University and Pepperdine University, and a PhD from Stanford University. He started his teaching career as a high school English teacher at Overfelt High School in San Jose, California. His professional roles have included fourth grade teacher; high school teacher; director of a small, experimental public high school; high school vice principal; continuation school principal; university professor; university director of secondary education; social science/teacher education division chair; director of the dean's honors program; and professor of great books. He is the recipient of the Harriet and Charles Luckman Distinguished Teacher Award and the Sigma Chi Omicron Professor of the Year Award. He has had the great fortune to have studied with John Daly, Alice Coleman, Lewis Owen, Al Grommon, Royce Clark, Elizabeth Cohen, David Tyack, Fannie Shaftel, Arturo Pacheco, Decker Walker, Elliot Eisner, and to have taught with Monte Steadman, Patricia Aboud, Joe Randazzo, Larry Giacomino, Nick Leon, Art Walsh, Mike McDermit, JoAnn Taylor, Bob Sexton, and Jim McGoldrick and to have had much better students than he could possibly have deserved. He has elementary, secondary, and community college teaching credentials and supervision and administrative credentials for K-12. He has written in the areas of curriculum, teaching, administration, and educational change for journals, including *Teacher Education Quarterly, Educational Leadership, Journal of Curriculum and Supervision, High School Journal, Record, Thrust,* and *California English.* He still collects baseball cards. He set out to become a superintendent and ended up as a college professor. Since he was 9 years old, he has known his career goal: to pitch for the Dodgers.

1

Creating the Game Plan

What is gamesmanship? Most difficult of questions to answer briefly. "The art of winning games without actually cheating" —that is my personal "working definition."
(Potter, 1931, p. 15)

Nobody ever said, "Work ball!" They say, "Play ball!" To me that means having fun.
(Willie Stargell in Freeman, 1996, p. 26)

This section defines the game plan and the gamesmanship that goes into effective teaching. It includes an explanation of the game plan; a discussion of putting on your game face—creating a favorable impression in getting a job and getting off to a quick start at your school and in your classroom; and remarks on the context of your school and cultural pluralism. The chapter also offers a stereotypical coach's pep talk; briefly describes the conditions of teaching that often have a great effect on the teacher's aptitude for enjoying this profession; and ends with miscellaneous tips for establishing yourself at your school.

Introducing the Game Plan

"Why must the teacher play this adversary role?" they asked. "Why can't he relax and enjoy his students?" Each question carries its own curious assumption. The first implies that the

Figure 1.1. Creating the Game Plan

role of the leader and guide amounts to the same thing as the role of the enemy, which on the face of it strains common sense. The second implies that if the teacher is a successful leader and guide, he automatically forfeits enjoyment. Not only is this last assumption false, its exact reverse is more likely to be true. Our enjoyment of any activity is enhanced when we know we're good at it. (Gray, 1969, p. 26).

I have always wanted to see the playbook for a professional football team. I have read that these books contain all a team's offensive and defensive plays, and that there is huge fine for any player who loses or photocopies that playbook. I would like this book to offer to teachers such valuable plans. I hope that you will pick up this book, smell the pages, look forward with excitement to the new season. As the season progresses, I hope that this book will come to have the coffee stains, ink smears, and dog-eared pages that prove its value.

I especially enjoy likening the approach of this book on teaching to the football coach's game plan, and this book purports to have most of the offensive and defensive plays that might be used in a school season. I hope that this playbook will be a resource you can refer to often to remind you of the variety of moves available to you as a teacher. I hope that the observations on teaching will help you to develop the necessary gamesmanship, good humor, goodwill, tough-mindedness, and resolve to succeed as a teacher, as well as provide the realization that you must constantly revise your own game plan to stay ahead of your students as they in turn change their strategies and responses to your teaching. Do keep in mind, however, that this must be a friendly competition, perhaps something like an all-star game, where you hope to elicit both your best performance and your students' best performance. Also, remember that while trying to create peak performance, you may not be smiling, but you should be having fun.

I have chosen the game plan metaphor for a number of reasons. One of the most important is that it suggests teaching can be fun. If you have played any game or sport, you know full well that you can have a huge frown on your face and yet be having the time of your life. A healthy sense of competition can be invigorating. Further, there is a necessary competitiveness not so much between you and individual students, although that will sometimes occur too, but between you and the class. Students need a contest, a match, an event, a test to grow. As teacher, you play a major role in giving students someone to grapple with so that they can both test and improve their developing strengths. Just like you write their exams, you are in a very real sense their test, their opportunity to improve their play. In turn, you will grow as a teacher and as a person.

The sense of competition that I want to foster here is related to the Greek sense of competition, *agron*. The true purpose of competition is to improve individual performance. It is not really about winning and losing. This game plan is about enjoying your role as teacher. Although it might be disastrous for you to lose a major class conflict, the intent is to avoid those kind of competitions. Your gamesmanship is in recognizing that students will test you and then turning that energy to their academic and personal growth. Your challenge is to influence the tardy student to be on time, the promising student to achieve, the dependent student to become more independent. This requires great skill on your part and gamesmanship. Be a player! Perform well! Have fun! But don't keep score. The only tally I suggest that you keep is whether you've made some sort of personal connection with each student each week. Beliefs, talent, skill are only

Figure 1.2. A healthy sense of competition can be invigorating.

as strong as they have been tested. Students only learn from teachers with whom they feel connected. You must challenge and connect.

Inevitably, someone will object that my use of the game plan metaphor does not treat teaching with the seriousness that it deserves. Inevitably, after reading about my observations on the games kids play in the classroom, someone will object that I am overly cynical about students. Competitor that I am, I will match the teacher evaluations that I have received from my students with those of anyone. Competitor that I am, I add that one cannot gain the highest student evaluations without thoroughly challenging the best students, protecting the supposed "weak" students, and making sure that every student simultaneously learns and appreciates the quality of life in the classroom. Good gamesmanship is no less serious than other approaches to teaching, but it also celebrates that teaching can be fun. Let me once again emphasize that my idea of gamesmanship is not about the teacher winning and the students losing (or vice versa). My approach does, however, accept that there is a necessary contest between students and their teacher,

Creating the Game Plan 5

Figure 1.3. There is a necessary contest between students and their teacher.

and that the better this is understood, the greater the prospect of learning by the students and a rewarding career for the teacher will be.

So, what's the basic game plan beyond the gamesmanship? In the ensuing sections of this book, I emphasize variety in teaching strategies that reach students as well as teach a subject matter's main skill areas. I emphasize avoiding discipline problems as much as possible by running a strong curriculum and having well-conceived expectations and procedures. When discipline problems do occur, I recommend a teacher's variation of the divide-and-conquer strategy. I advocate that teaching and discipline be handled as multicultural education and that the key to multicultural education is appreciating differences and diversifying instruction. These are the basics of the game plan.

Putting on Your Game Face

Be on time. Bust your butt. Play smart. And have some laughs along the way.

(Whitey Herzog in Freeman, 1996, p. 26)

As a playbook, this book is primarily about teaching in the classroom. As the Reverend Jesse Jackson once said, however, a text without a context is a pretext. Your job, your classroom, your students, exist within the context of a school. A few preliminary preparations can help you immeasurably to create the opportunity and space to do your best work.

Getting the Teaching Job

First, if you have not done so already, you actually need to get that teaching job. I have often marveled that my own student teachers plan to spend less time on their candidacy for a teaching job than they spend on any term paper. What are they thinking? As my friend and former student Bob Escudero often tells his own students, failing to prepare is preparing to fail. You need to spend quality time working to get the right job. As a former high school administrator hiring new teachers, I found it almost inexplicable that out of 100 applicants for a teaching position, it was rare to have 5 with what I would consider to be full applications. The good news is that, if you are thorough, you should get a lot of interviews and job offers.

I encourage my own student teachers to do at least five things:

1. Complete the school district's application form.
2. Include a very professional looking vita/resume with your application.
3. Send your placement file (usually from your college's placement office), which should include a minimum of three letters of recommendation that you are confident are strong.
4. Send a personal letter to each of the respective districts or schools to which you apply indicating why you want to work at that particular school and district. (Frankly, administrators rarely pay attention to applications that look like they have been sent just anywhere.)
5. Visit the school site (this can be tricky). Go to the administration office, ask for the principal's secretary. Tell that person your name, that you are a candidate for a teaching job, that you do not expect to be seen by anyone, but that you do want to walk around the campus to get a feel for the school.

If you ask to see a school administrator, a good principal's secretary should tell you no. There are official procedures for screening candidates. If you ask to walk around the campus, however, you will get a feel for the school; if you make a good impression, the secretary will mention your name to a vice principal or principal. There is an excellent chance that administrator will take a look at your application (and leave it right on top of the stack). You may even meet a key teacher, department chair, or administrator, merely from a brief visit. Your visit shows that you are thorough and clearly interested in their school.

My friend and former student, Damian Jenkins, recommends a sixth step. She advises candidates to call the principal's secretary a couple of days later to say thank you. If you hit it off with that person, you might want to call later to find out where the selection process stands. Damian was the most thorough of anyone I have ever known in her pursuit of her first teaching job, and she was offered the most number of jobs of anyone I have ever known.

A final note in this regard: If you are offered a job you might take, but you are still a candidate for a job elsewhere that you prefer, tell the school that offered you a job that you are thrilled by its offer, you want to talk to your significant others, and what is the deadline for your official answer? Then you can call the school you prefer, assure them that you are not in anyway trying to pressure them but that it is the only job you prefer to the one you have been offered, and will they know about whether you will hear if you will be offered a job there before the other school's deadline? Under these circumstances, a school principal may be able to hasten the process if it seems you are the candidate the school wants. You may be offered this job as well. If not, you haven't started out on the wrong foot at the other school by having announced that it is second choice.

Interviewing

You should naturally get better as you undergo more interviews. But you don't want to be still practicing interviews at the jobs you most want. Thus, don't hesitate to apply for a lot of jobs; you will be surprised how much more attractive any job looks when the school says that it would like you to work there. This increased number of probable interviews will improve your chances at doing better with each subsequent interview.

When you do get an interview, it is always helpful to obtain some inside information. For example, you might find out the school especially needs someone to work with the incoming ninth graders, someone with special enthusiasm for helping them adjust to high school. Such information can help you with the interview.

At the interview, the interview committee may be small or large. Ordinarily, it will include a school administrator, a department chair, and another teacher. Sometimes it will include a parent and/or a student. Without going into all the questions the committee might ask you, it will almost always ask you to summarize your school background. Do so concisely and to your best advantage. Don't assume that members will remember what is in your application.

You can also expect to be asked about your strengths and your weaknesses. (The best answer to the weakness question is usually that you work too hard, at the expense of your social life.)

You will often be asked at the end of the interview whether you have any further questions. Do not ask a question you can find out elsewhere, such as what's the salary schedule or when does the committee expect to decide. This is often a good time to say that you are anxious to be a part of the school community and to ask about what opportunities you might have to coach, or work with a club, or start a new program.

A tip: For some reason, during an interview there will usually be one question that you are answering badly. Your tendency will be to keep talking, digging yourself into a bigger hole. Instead of continuing, stop, say that you aren't happy with how you are answering this question, and ask whether you might start over or have a different question. This shows presence of mind, not weakness. But you should do this only once during any given interview.

What is the interview committee looking for in this interview? Besides looking for someone who will fit in with the school staff, it will have two primary and somewhat competing concerns. Invariably, someone on the interview committee will be concerned that you will be academically demanding as a teacher and can handle discipline problems well. Someone else will be concerned that you will relate well with students, that you will be student-centered, that you will motivate students, that school will be more enjoyable because you are there. You need to speak to both concerns in your interview. Indeed, this is perhaps the key challenge in teaching. Can you be firm and fair? Can you be demanding and respected? Can you work your students and still have some fun? This book should help you gain the confidence to balance both these expectations and demands. Make sure you show this ability in your interview.

Your interviewers will undoubtedly ask you a question about how you would handle a discipline problem. I was once asked what I'd do if I encountered two students having sex on campus. This could happen, I suppose, but it has never happened to me or anyone I know.

What I should have realized was that it is common to be asked a tough question because the committee may want to see how the interviewee reacts to pressure. Staying calm is essential. A good way to handle such a hypothetical question may be to say that you aren't entirely sure, but that it may be helpful to explain how you have handled a particularly difficult situation. Then give the committee a specific sample of a discipline situation you do think you handled well, even if it was in a role other than a teacher's role.

Finally, I will say that I did not respond to interviews as well as I would have liked. I always felt like I was on trial, and I worked too hard at the accuracy of my answers. The best interviewees I have seen spend nearly as much time connecting with those who are doing the interviews, even asking them questions. The more you can make the interview a conversation, the better.

Making a Good Impression as a Rookie

Like a professional athlete, you will need a "game face." It will help show that you mean business, that you are committed to being successful. The game face that you choose should help you focus and concentrate on the job at hand. This game face will also cue students as to their own roles. If they cannot recognize how you intend to play the game, they will probably become very frustrated not knowing how to respond to your expectations.

Before I describe some of the more obvious and popular roles teachers take, I will assume that most of you are just beginning as teachers. Thus, your status as a rookie has its own liabilities. First, as a rookie, you will likely be given what the other teachers consider to be the most difficult teaching assignment in your department. Those with seniority will have assuredly looked out for themselves. Your tough assignment is seen as part of paying your dues. At least until recently, the rookies in professional sports literally carried the baggage of the more experienced players during road trips. You aren't likely to be hazed by the other teachers, but they will be watching, and you will need some friends on campus to ensure that you have the support necessary to develop as a new teacher.

So what's the best game face for a new teacher? Eager and earnest are good places to start. Although I emphasize that you must find out what curricular materials and discipline strategies work for you, make a point to find out what other teachers do particularly well, and ask them about it. "What do you do when a student forgets to bring the textbook?" "What's a short story or film that works with most students?" "What particulars do you expect students to memorize?" Because it is essential to project an aura of competence, such questions should reflect that you are trying to refine your game plan, not find one. Experienced teachers will be pleased and impressed that you asked.

Roles to Choose or Adapt

You should also think about some of the more obvious roles you can use as you wade through your choices of long-term game faces. Although over the period of a year you may become appreciated for your individuality, there are some basic teacher types or roles that you can take advantage of so that students can more readily recognize basic expectations. Sometimes these roles are played in combinations. For example, I like to parlay a combination of the intellectual and the coach to try to cajole high academic performance. A basic list of roles includes the following:

- The artiste
- The governor
- The intellectual
- The scientist
- The surrogate parent
- The CEO
- The saint
- The coach

The Artiste

Typically, the artistes drive peculiar cars and wear artsy clothes. They are "into" their work and see their class as their medium. They have great confidence in their work, more or less regardless of what their students might otherwise think. The suitable pressure the artistes put on their students is that the students' own work may be put on public display in front of their peers, and the students are not likely to feel as comfortable with this attention as the artiste.

The Governor

Often, but certainly not only social studies teachers, the governors are likely to see all aspects of classroom behavior as their domain. Rules are to be followed or changed. Students must be made to see their civic, classroom responsibilities. The governors like to point out that "no man (sic) is an island unto himself," and perhaps that this is a John Donne quote, not Ernest Hemingway, and that the point is well taken even if it is no longer politically correct. The suitable pressure the governors place on students is that the students are included in the decisions about the class, so they have an investment in the class.

The Intellectual

Students always suspect that the intellectuals' mothers must have laid out their clothes each morning. The intellectuals prefer polysyllabic words to clear communication. The suitable pressure intellectuals place on their students is that the intellectual students want to match wits with them, and the other students are afraid they will miss something they should have been paying attention to.

The Scientist

The scientists usually seem to care the least about their personal appearance. In the old days, they all wore funny shoes. Now they mostly wear Rockports or Timberlands. The suitable pressure scientists put on students is that the scientist has the technical knowledge that will appear on tests, and this is also the hardest knowledge to get someone else to explain.

The Surrogate Parent

The surrogate parents want to nurture students. Sometimes this can be annoying to students. Someone usually brings these teachers apples. Other students may resent the intrusion on their independence. The suitable pressure surrogate parents place on students is that the students recognize they can never have enough people looking out for them, so don't burn this bridge, or teacher.

The CEO

The CEOs can tell students the first day of class how many points it will take to earn an A. The remainder of the year is spent organizing tests, quizzes, papers, and presentations that give students the opportunity to earn all these points. It is a matter of productivity. The suitable pressure CEOs put on students is that students know a missed opportunity in February can haunt them in June.

The Saint

There is usually no more than one of these per school. The saint is usually a single person. The saint devotes his or her life to the school. Some students take advantage of the saint. The suitable pressure on students is that other students often feel obliged to protect the saint, if only because they owe the saint some borrowed money.

The Coach

Coaches specialize in strategy and motivation. They tend to know all the tricks and shortcuts for mastering a subject. They spend a lot of time threatening, cajoling, badgering, instigating, and prodding students. The suitable pressure coaches place on students is that this role is the one where students feel that the teacher is on their side, while still recognizing that they are independent, individuating adolescents.

Why does it seem I am poking some fun at these positive roles? Although these roles can be very useful, they should always be played with a sense of humor and the realization that only by infusing them with your own life force will they work. I also feel that the best teachers can act out any of these roles and still others according to their students' needs. These roles call out, "play me, or trade me."

~ Contextualizing Your Game Plan

A text without a context is a pretext.
(Reverend Jesse Jackson)

The School Context

Having secured that first contract (and don't assume you have a job until you have a signed contract—superintendents and school boards have been known to change staffing policies so that offers are not confirmed with a contract), you will have some concerns about how you fit into the school's culture. Rightly or wrongly, you will create an impression that will influence the support you receive as a new teacher. Rightly or wrongly, you are not likely to have more than two official classroom visits by a school administrator any year that you teach. So, to my mind, you have to be very careful about what the school grapevine has to say about you. Some people may argue that worrying about your image shouldn't be necessary. Well, for most of us mere mortals, it is. The following tips should help you choose an effective game face, manage the impression you make, and get off to a good start. If you spend some additional time thinking about the tips, you should gain some additional insight into how school cultures tend to work.

Be early, never late. Pick up your mail first so the principal, who checks mail boxes for such information, will know that you are there. Never lose your keys! Be nice to the principal's secretary! Be nice to the custodians! Do a general clean-up of your room every day so that the word going back to the main office is that you must be in control of your classroom. Go to the most visible of the school's extracurricular activities! Carry a few extra dollars each week to buy the candy, ribbons, balloons students inevitably are selling. It's the least the new teacher can do, even though he or she is lowest on the salary schedule. Try to find a mentor, an older teacher or librarian, who can give you tips and appreciate your effort. My only negative tip is to make only *in*frequent visits to the teacher lounge. For whatever reason, every teacher's lounge I've ever visited attracts the school's most negative teachers. Do visit every once in a while as a professional courtesy. Never when you are feeling down. Ask everyone there if they think you are grading too hard, regardless of how high your grades actually are, and then find a safer haven for most of your lunches. If you do get trapped into one of those negative teacher lounge encounters, I have found that it is quite fun to surprise the teacher complaining about how bad school is by telling him or her that the research shows that things are actually a lot worse than he or she thinks. It confuses the heck out of that person. . . .

The Context of Cultural Pluralism

The image of the melting pot doesn't work. It has been replaced by the image of the salad bowl, where each element is still itself, but contributes to the whole.
(Arturo Pacheco, multicultural education class at Stanford University, 1978)

I consider the issues surrounding cultural pluralism, multiethnic education, and cultural diversity supremely important. There is no other issue in education I consider more important or more worthy of in-depth study, analysis, and conversation. When it comes to the

14 CREATING A WINNING GAME PLAN

Figure 1.4. A major theme of this book: Appreciate differences, diversify instruction.

individual classroom, however, I have reached a conclusion that I truly believe gets at the very essence of multicultural education. It is a major theme of this entire book. It is simply this: Appreciate differences, diversify instruction.

Your life will be richer if you spend the rest of your days learning about the different ethnic groups of our pluralistic society. The best way to learn what you need to know about each of your students will be from your students. You will invariably get students from backgrounds you do not know anything about. And, there is more diversity within groups than between groups. For example, no matter how well a particular group has done on the SAT math section, your particular student may have trouble with fractions. No matter which ethnic group has done best in this event in the Olympics, your student may hate that sport. No matter what dishes a group may be famous for, your student may never eat that food. No matter how important you do or do not think ethnic identity should be to the individual, your student will have his or her own ideas. As a teacher in a classroom of 25-40 students, you will be well served if you appreciate differences and diversify instruction.

Simultaneously, if not paradoxically, you need to acquire knowledge about social class, sex, race, ethnicity, and "handicaps," and you can then ignore all this knowledge with regard to your students. Knowledge about differences opens us up to the full range of human possibilities; the concept of normal distribution reminds us that any given individual may not fit any of the tendencies (or stereotypes) for his or her categories, such as social class, sex, and race.

The presumption of normal distribution is that with regard to height, weight, intelligence, vertical leap, and math aptitude, most people are grouped near the average. A recent movie had the dubious title *White Men Can't Jump*. At this time it is fact, not a racist observation, that African American men are overrepresented in the National Basketball Association (NBA) per their percentage of the American population, and that most NBA players are distinguished by both height and leaping ability. But the key issue for a teacher of 30-35 students from a U.S. population of over 250 million to understand is that even if the overall normal distribution curve of African American men was found to be higher than that of other Americans, and that the top half of 1% of this group tended to excel above all other groups (regardless why there might be a superiority in ability), it is still quite possible that an African American male might be the worst at the vertical leap in a teacher's random group of 30-35 students. *There is much more difference within groups than between groups.*

In a PE course, the teacher must never presume which students are the best at the vertical leap, nor who might improve the most. One of my all-time best students, who went on to become a teacher himself, is Japanese American and a musician/music major. One would have to be immune to culture not to have heard about the success of Japanese Americans in math and engineering. So, in a class discussion about stereotypes and normal distribution curves, the class asked John about the messages he had heard in school. John reported that teachers and counselors alike had encouraged him in math and science, and only one high school music teacher had believed him when he said he wanted to go to college and study music. Even if there is a tendency for some groups to excel in certain fields, that is useless information for understanding a sample size of 30-35 students.

As I argued earlier, what the knowledge of differences in tendencies among age, social class, sex, race, religion, ethnic groups can best do is alert the teacher to the variety of talents and needs of all students.

The lesson of the self-fulfilling prophecy is that we tend to expect more of students most like us, and students rise to those expectations. Thus, it is of paramount importance to see what is of value in each and every student.

All you can truly count on in your class of 30-35 students is that each student is likely to be very different and that you need to be open to those differences to teach effectively. And why wouldn't you want to learn as much as possible about every ethnic or other kind of group? It will enrich your life. But my advice is so strong I think of it as a truism—for all you learn, do not make any presumptions about the individuals in your classroom. Baseball players Jackie Robinson and Maury Wills were two of the heroes of my youth. Robinson emphasized his ethnic identity as a vital part of who he was; Wills emphasized his individuality. Those two positions are often thought of as liberal and conservative, yet it was Robinson who was an active Republican. While learning all you can about all the earth's peoples, let your students disclose themselves how they define who they are.

As I've said, cultural tendencies aren't all that helpful predicting individual behavior—there's more difference in groups than between groups. I'll admit that in my own personally constructed ideal world, we would be color-blind. Early in my teaching career, I asked a "boxboy" at my grocer where to turn in bottles and was directed to a line in the liquor department. When I finally got to my turn, the clerk was annoyed and wanted to know which boxboy had given me such egregious misinformation. I turned to finger the culprit. There were three boxboys in the store. I never presume to know what ethnic identification an individual lays claim to, but it appeared that one was African American, one Hispanic, and one Asian. I didn't know which person I had spoken to. I lost points with myself on being unable to recognize a person I'd spoken to, but gave myself points for at least being color blind.

Anyway, in my ideal world, we would live up to Martin Luther King's dream of being judged strictly by the content of our character. In the meantime, demographic categories are helpful when they point out groups that are not represented or are underrepresented in our programs and institutions. Given the concept of normal distribution, there is no true reason to exclude anyone from any opportunity, and diversity provides a wider talent pool and more perspective. By appreciating differences and diversifying instruction, each of our students may feel a vital part of the whole and better learn areas of both strength and weakness for a better lifelong placement in an area of proven interest.

There is no substitute for empathy for each student. Here I make the distinction between sympathy and empathy—perhaps no one wants pity so much as an empathetic walking in one's shoes. For a teacher, empathy starts with an openness of heart and mind, a willingness to grasp strengths and weaknesses while staying focused on inherent worth and future potential. I wish for you that you have been and will be "adopted" by a rainbow coalition of parents and students who will teach you to see in a kaleidoscope of opportunities. My first year of teaching, I was "adopted" by a family of a different ethnic group than my own, and their love, sharing, pointing out, nourishment of the body and soul, and recommended readings, movies, and concerts blessed me richly. Empathy, understanding, and confidence are essentials to good teaching. I think it is great advice to appreciate differences and diversify instruction, but it is only through truly caring about that individual student who truly is the heart of the academic enterprise, who may otherwise tend to drive you crazy, that you will truly become a great teacher.

The Pep Talk

A life isn't significant except for its impact on other lives.
(Jackie Robinson in Freeman, 1996, p. 39)

I am over 50 years old, and even I'm too old to remember Notre Dame's legendary football coach, Knute Rockne, much less the movie that starred Ronald Reagan. But I have heard of the famous halftime speech, "win one for the Gipper," and here is my take on the speech that reputedly motivated Notre Dame to come back from a huge deficit and beat its arch rival, Army. Enjoy.

Failing to prepare is preparing to fail. Stand and deliver. Be resourceful. Be a player. Speak softly and carry a big stick. Win one for the Gipper. Climb every mountain, forge every stream. Dare to be different. When the going gets tough, the tough get going. Do something important with your life—Teach!

Don't be an idiot! Why do so many teachers seem to have absolutely no recollection of what it was like to be a student—good and bad? I am sometimes dumbfounded at what teachers will try to make work in the classroom. I visited a struggling English teacher who was teaching relative pronouns to ninth graders in "dumbbell" English. I have a strong sense of my own ability as a teacher, and I would never have been able to pull off teaching relative pronouns to that particular class at that time. (I do have some great short stories that would probably have worked. . . .)

Teaching is great sport! One-hundred and fifty students trying deliberately to drive you crazy while you just want to pass Go and collect $200. Can you defy the odds and make a class smile at 8 a.m.? Can you teach the same prep a third time and get something new out of the lesson? Can you find a book for Abigail that will become the first book she has ever read? Can you find something for Stan to do before you kill him? What is the record number of interruptions during a single class period? Is it possible to go an entire period without talking? Can you really make students love Silas Marner? Is it possible to teach and have a social life? There's no board game or video game with the complexities and challenges. So, play smart! Pay attention to the answers along the way. Let failure steel your will. Don't forget to smell the roses along the way. Be a conqueror. The best thing since sliced bread. Have a game plan and a game face.

Support the people who support you. Do the right thing. Commit yourself to each student while knowing full well you can never truly get to know most of your students. Teach stuff that is important, but that you also care about. Have enough meaningful stuff to engage them. When it comes to discipline, unless it is a completely unexpected direct assault on your authority, handle it one on one. Try to remember something of what it was like to be a kid, and for goodness sake, recognize the games students will try to play with you. It's their job. They won't know their limits unless someone tests them, and they will not learn to act independently unless they challenge adult expectations. Whew! You yourself got through all that as a student; you still want to teach! Respond now firmly, fairly, good naturedly! Don't take stuff that's not personal personally!

Get centered. Have the right attitude. Work hard; play hard. I repeat, be smart! The following pages will help you develop your own game plan and make you more savvy. Write in the margins of this book, tear out the stuff you don't like, add your own material. As you determine and set your own game plan, as you organize a curriculum that will engage students, as you set expectations and procedures for their behavior and implement a range of discipline strategies, it will all be for naught if you do not play with smartness, enthusiasm, and heart! And while for all your Herculean efforts the best that you can hope for is that some of your students will be slightly better people, celebrate that you will have become a much better person, a more talented, open, resilient, interested, interesting, human being.

Like a great athlete, the plan is nothing until the execution. Like it is for a great athlete, the thrill of a stellar performance can hardly be described. Like it is for a great athlete, the fun is often in the work and concentration. Unlike it is for a great athlete, we are gradually changing the world into a better place to live. *Teach.* It is both a verb and an affectionate title of respect. Break a leg.

Conditions of Teaching

But I go down to my classroom. Room 33. Inside it, I close the door, and all of the above, most every concern brought up in this book, falls away.
(Herndon, 1985, p. 156)

Having blown my bugle call to teaching, I do need to offer a warning. Although teaching is a profession for people of goodwill, not all people of goodwill are necessarily cut out for teaching. There are conditions that mitigate against success that some handle better than others.

For as long as I can remember, I have thought that there are only three prominent jobs one could do that are so intrinsically worthwhile one need not justify the career choice: ministry, medicine, and teaching. By the way, I have discovered that a poll indicates that the American public rates these three professions, in that order, as the three professions contributing the most to the public good (see Gose, 1985). Elsewhere, I'll write about the worth of teaching. I mention the value here as a preface to acknowledging certain hard realities of teaching in America. You'll never succeed or enjoy teaching unless you accommodate these realities. They form the stuff that create the burned-out teachers you complained so vociferously about as a student when you were going through school yourself.

One of the best student teachers I ever had, Judy Brown, summed up these realities: You are never prepared for the amount of failure you experience as a teacher. Repeat after me 10 times: You are never prepared for the amount of failure you experience as a teacher. You are never prepared for the amount of failure you experience as a teacher. You are never prepared for the amount of failure you experience as a teacher. You are never prepared for the amount of failure you experience as a teacher. You are never prepared for the amount of failure you experience as a teacher. You are never prepared for the amount of failure you experience as a teacher. You are never prepared for the amount of failure you experience as a teacher. You are never

Figure 1.5. What adult would work under such crowded conditions so amicably?

prepared for the amount of failure you experience as a teacher. You are never prepared for the amount of failure you experience as a teacher. You are never prepared for the amount of failure you experience as a teacher. Like gravity, failure in teaching is one of your primary limitations. (As I write this, I have a vision of Newton sitting under the tree waiting to discover gravity and being hit on the head by an apple that had otherwise been intended for a student to give to a teacher.) It may help you to accept a certain amount of inevitable failure if you think about some of the specific conditions of teaching.

First, 30-40 school-aged "children" were never meant to sit quietly for 6 hours in 900-1,200 square feet of space. What adult would work under such crowded conditions so amicably? Fast food kitchens are the only other major workplace with such crowded conditions, and at least those workers are able to move around to let off energy.

Second, research has shown that teachers must make about 1,000 different decisions a day (Jackson, 1968). These decisions range in importance from whether to acknowledge a raised hand to whether or not to let the "worst" student go to the restroom. Each of these choices requires energy and judgment. A teacher does not have to mess up many of those 1,000 decisions to have a very bad, horrible, no-good day.

Third, all those kids are a completely different age than yourself, and ordinarily there is no other adult in your classroom. Where else would you work with so little opportunity to share what's going on with a peer? This isolation takes a toll.

Fourth, schools are more about sorting and selection than about education. Although you will naturally want your students to love the subject matter as much as you do, 99.9% of them will decide they don't, nor will they go on to receive a bachelor's degree in your area of study. (It's why it is more important for you to cultivate a love of learning rather than a specific allegiance to your particular subject matter.)

Fifth, you will be subject to all the other natural laws, especially Murphy's law that anything that can go wrong, will. If only because of the four conditions just cited, the consequences of Murphy's law will be significant.

All the lessons of this book will not repeal these conditions of teaching, but they can help you get into condition to teach. Like yourself, each of your students starts the school day with the primary aim of successfully living out that day. It's not that subject matter isn't vitally important, nor that it doesn't deserve for you to teach it effectively, but you and your students will all be happier if you start out with the primary intention of having a good day.

Having both given you the pep talk to teach and emphasized the kind of conditions that are inherent limitations, the remainder of the book will be about creating the winning game plan, including planning your curriculum, handling discipline, and thriving in teaching. As said earlier, however, the game plan, playbook, or gamesmanship will not work if you do not play with heart. Thus, create a game plan that will work with your students and still allow you to enjoy teaching. The following pages should prove a good place to start.

Miscellaneous Tips on Establishing Yourself

I have always found lists helpful. The following is simply a long list of tips. These are the tips that I have had reason to pass on most often to new teachers. Many are repeated elsewhere in these pages. In this form, they are quick reminders and have greater prospect of being immediately useful. They are most likely to connect when they are answering a particular need. The key is their timeliness, so I have left them in what I hope is a useful list form. I think you will find that it is a good list to review periodically.

Tips About School Personnel

- Be nice to the secretaries, avoid the bus drivers, don't let your room get too messy. Those staff members are often the informal CIA and FBI. Your reputation may largely depend on what these people report informally to their supervisors and the public.
- Watch out for parking policies, coffee policies, and smoking policies. My recommendation is to park far away, don't drink coffee, and don't smoke. I've seen these issues dominate faculty meetings, conversations, and cliques. You can make a mortal enemy by parking in a secretary's parking spot. And no one ever agrees at any school on who is carrying the load of keeping coffee in the pot and the mugs cleaned up. Smokers versus non-smokers are like cats and dogs. These issues often are the sources of the deepest, unspoken resentments at school.
- If you absolutely need administrative help, use it. But administrators are exceedingly busy people too, and they want to feel that before they help you with an unusual problem, you are basically a competent person. Administrators often become defensive when you bring up a problem, because it usually means it will be time-consuming for them and probably impossible to solve anyway. So mention a problem (that unbeknownst to them you have already solved very successfully), watch them tense up defensively, and then share how you solved the problem. In their relief, they will be most congratulatory and supportive, you will have won points, and they will be less defensive and more helpful should you find a problem you really can't solve later.
- CYA. Cover your assets. It's helpful to know which on-site administrator you can best trust. If you hear a rumor that involves you, for example a student in your class was "seen" under the influence of alcohol, there's a good chance others have heard the rumor. I think it is wise to inform a trusted administrator informally something like, "I've heard a rumor

so-and-so was under the influence of alcohol in my class. I couldn't tell, but I'll continue to watch for a problem." This communicates that you are on top of things and, should the administration pick this rumor up elsewhere, you've helped them cover their assets.

- Games some faculty play. Although teachers are generally better off than they have been for the last three or four thousand years, working conditions have deteriorated for the first time in history over the past 10 to 20 years (real salary, class size, seriousness of student problems). But even before the slippage, there was something about teaching that attracted many chronic complainers. Such teachers especially enjoy sharing their complaints with new teachers and do so ad infinitum. I have found only one way to make interaction with such teachers tolerable—I play a game I call "It's Really a Lot Worse Than You Realize." It is a variation of a routine Monty Python has where the discussants (all dressed in tuxedoes) argue about who really had it worse growing up; the "winner" lived under the hole in the road. No matter how bleak a picture your chronically complaining fellow teacher paints, with a little imagination and real or imagined data, you can explain that things really are even worse than that person suspects, and explain why with an enigmatic smile.

- Because wizened and grizzled veteran teachers will invariably think you, as a beginning teacher, will be too easy on students, I highly recommend that you give them the respect that is their due and periodically seek their advice publicly, ordinarily in the faculty lounge, on whether, indeed, you are grading too hard, giving too many assignments, and lecturing too much, regardless of what you actually happen to be doing. This goes over much better than your explanations of how well your "new" ideas are working in your classroom.

Tips Regarding Students Outside of Class

- Attend students' extracurricular activities. Go to the games, the club activities, the dances, the award ceremonies, the talent shows. Compliment students for work well done.
- Even when you can't go, pay attention to the extracurricular events on campus and acknowledge students for their efforts.

- Make 'em go home reciting Shakespeare. It's good PR, and every student knows it's not only part of our cultural heritage but what every "good" school makes our students learn. Do, however, pick a good passage that's not too long.

Tips About Your Relationship With Students

- The only way to have a happy and worthwhile teaching career is to teach students, not subject matter. With all the time I have spent in school, I hope I do not have to explain that I think that subject matter is incredibly important. But if you are letting any particular subject stand between you and your students, you won't have any fun, you'll be frustrated all the time, and teaching will get worse each year instead of better. Get on the students' side; you can still give the As to those who do the best in the subject; but you can truly like all your students regardless of how much they like what you are teaching.

- You have spent your entire life getting clear on your likes and dislikes, preferences and peeves. Now FORGET those distinctions! Now you must learn to appreciate differences; it will be especially useful to cultivate an appreciation for the odd. Not one kid in your classroom will be like you think a person should be; the most odd kid is potentially your most difficult problem. If you stick to your own time-proven biases, you will be one unhappy turkey.

- Somewhat to my surprise, I have found that every kid is interested in something that I find interesting. I was so surprised by this, that I developed a theory that it was true for every kid. And then I met Spanky. Spanky was a real test. Mostly he was an incredibly boring person, taking up space. My initial efforts to prod him into doing something, anything, led me to discover that what few personality traits he had were all negative. He was disloyal to his few friends, had a negative attitude toward seemingly everything, was the prototypical party pooper. After several weeks, I even mentioned to a colleague that my theory about all students having at least one redeemable quality was wrong. And then, to my astonishment, because I had otherwise already concluded that Spanky had the IQ of an amoeba, I found out that Spanky could quote long sections of dialogue from classic movies. Seems he stayed up very late at night watching old movies on TV. I had started teaching a film class when my wife told me that because I couldn't go 5 minutes talking to anyone without talking about movies, at least my students could get credit for it. Here, to my great surprise, it turned out that one of the most disagreeable people I had ever met had a love for movies and knew the old ones better than I did. It was a starting place.

- On becoming a teacher: In working with student teachers over the past years, I have identified two factors that are sometimes difficult for them to manage in moving from the student role to the teacher role. First, students have spent their entire lives getting clear on who they are, what their values are, and how those standards are the way things should be. They have established personal identity. Then as teachers, that whole process is in direct conflict with the demands placed on the teacher. The teacher who persists in expecting students to be like he or she was is lost. Now the task is to appreciate differences. No matter how well conceived your values are, kids will be different and you must cultivate your appreciation of those differences. (A corollary to this is that most teachers also need to cultivate that personal identity into greater personality to be effective with kids.)
- New teachers spend their educational careers being sorted and selected into their favorite academic area. Expecting all one's students to appreciate your subject matter would in reality be counterproductive. Society does not have room for your entire class to pursue your level of expertise in your subject matter. Some kids are there to learn it's *not* what they want to spend a lot of time with in their lives. So, if you see yourself as a subject matter specialist, you are probably in serious trouble. The better advice is to help students appreciate something about your subject. But you should not take it all personally, rather cultivate your appreciation of your own dramatic performance in the role of teacher. As such, you can feign indignation, wrath, disgust, or mirth as necessary and appropriate; do a great job; and go home happy that you handled 99% of the average teaching day's interactions effectively. It's an acquired trait you must develop to become a truly effective teacher year after year.

2

Planning Lessons and Teaching Strategies

This chapter has seven subchapters. The first looks at what to teach. The second looks at the variety of teaching techniques and strategies available. The third looks at organizing and pacing the curriculum. The fourth looks at grading and evaluation. The fifth looks at motivation. The sixth is a list of miscellaneous tips about successful teaching. The seventh is about teaching the so-called hidden curriculum.

I intend this book to be a game plan and a playbook. I have tried to include anything that might be helpful to getting a good start as a teacher. The section on what to teach is comparable to including the rule book within a sport's playbook. I think the College Board (1983) has done a masterful job of outlining basic subjects in such a concise way as to make them immediately accessible for the novice teacher, immediately practical for assuring that the subject matter basics are being addressed.

~ What to Teach: The Basic Outline of Subjects

> *What was it that everyone in America could agree on that kids needed to learn? Your decision has got to be in terms of what everyone in the community already knows—what The People know.*
>
> (Herndon, 1971, p. 129)

Figure 2.1. What was it that everyone in America could agree on that kids needed to learn?

This book emphasizes the basics. The College Board's (1983) outline of the basic academic subjects is manageable for the beginning teacher. You should not fail to look over your district's course of study and the state framework for your subject, however.

Having made that recommendation, I am confident you will recognize the economy, practicality, manageability, and utility of the College Board's (1983) outline. This outline becomes the reference for the sample lesson plan formats included in the Resources section. Please check out your own subject matter in this outline and evaluate whether anything basic is missing.

My problem with most curricular frameworks is that they cover too much territory to be practical in either planning or explaining to students or parents what about your subject matter you are trying to teach. (By the way, I was an English teacher who admits that I did not spend a lot of time trying to teach relative pronouns to ninth graders.) You may be well versed in John Donne's metaphysical conceits, but most of your students are not likely to share such an interest. I like Jim Herndon's rule of thumb on what should be taught—what the people know. I once had my roommate, who was an attorney, grade my

English class's essays. I was not terribly surprised that he was able to give my students the exact same grades that I had. The important stuff, and skills, to teach are what other educated people know. Emphasize that and eschew the esoteric.) Anyway, most curricular frameworks have far too many details to keep in mind. Which is why I have included the College Board's (1983) outline of basic academic subjects. The College Board spent millions of dollars figuring out what there is in each subject that students need for college. That's a good place to start with what you should be teaching, and the best part is that the list for each subject area can be captured in less than a page of print! When your principal, department chair, precocious student, or parent asks why the heck you have your students reading an article in the sports section of your local paper, you can answer, "Because I am having them recognize the intention of (the writer) like the people at College Board expect, and of course it is also a part of the district's approved curriculum framework, it's just easier to explain to students in terms of the benefit the assignment will have for them if they do go on to college...."

The only change that I would make in the College Board's (1983) text is that I think the outline applies to all students, not just the college bound. In fact, many of the students who do not go on to college immediately after high school will eventually go back. Even if they do not, they deserve to be taught the best skills of the respective academic subjects.

The College Board's Outline of the Basic Academic Subjects

Following is a reprint of the outline of the basic academic subjects students should study in high school, issued as part of the College Board's (1983) statement on academic preparation for college.[1]

Study in the basic academic subjects provides the detailed knowledge and skills necessary for effective work in college. Students who intend to go to college will need this basic learning in order to obtain the full benefits of higher education. This learning provides the foundation for college study in all fields.

For successful college work in certain fields, students will need more than this basic learning. This chapter also outlines the more extensive learning necessary for study in those fields....

The knowledge and skills needed for college are outcomes of secondary school study.

Planning Lessons and Teaching Strategies   29

Figure 2.2. What should be taught?

These outcomes can be achieved in a variety of ways. Consequently, although *Academic Preparation for College* (College Board, 1983) is intended to provide a framework for designing secondary school curricula, this chapter itself does not describe such curricula. It does not give specific course titles and contents. It goes beyond prescribing years of study to describe what students actually need to learn as a result of their study. It outlines the knowledge and skills that students will need in order to have a fair chance of getting full value from their college education. . . .

English

Reading and Literature

- The ability to read critically by asking pertinent questions about what they have read, by recognizing assumptions and implications, and by evaluating ideas

- The ability to read a literary text analytically, seeing relationships between form and content
- The ability to read with understanding a range of literature, rich in quality and representative of different literary forms and various cultures
- Interest in and a sense of inquiry about certain works
- The ability to respond actively and imaginatively to literature

Writing

- The recognition that writing is a process involving a number of elements, including collecting information and formulating ideas, determining their relationship, drafting, arranging paragraphs in an appropriate order and building transitions between them, and revising what has been written
- The ability to write as a way of discovering and clarifying ideas
- The ability to write appropriately for different occasions, audiences, and purposes (persuading, explaining, describing, telling a story)
- Skill and assurance in using the conventions of standard written English

Speaking and Listening

- The ability to engage in discussion as both speaker and listener—interpreting, analyzing, and summarizing
- The ability to contribute to classroom discussions in a way that is readily understood by listeners—that is, succinct and to the point
- The ability to present an opinion persuasively
- The ability to recognize the intention of a speaker and to be aware of the techniques a speaker is using to affect an audience
- The ability to recognize and take notes on important points in lectures and discussions
- The ability to question inconsistency in logic and to separate fact from opinion

Language

College entrants will also need to understand in some depth the following principles concerning the English language:

- English . . . operates according to grammatical systems and patterns of usage
- English continues to undergo change
- English is influenced by other languages both ancient and modern
- English has several levels of usage, and consequently the language appropriate in some situations may not be appropriate in others
- English has many dialects
- English words, like those of other languages, gather meaning from their context and carry connotations

The Arts

Students going to college will profit from the following preparation in the arts:

- The ability to understand and appreciate the unique qualities of each of the arts
- The ability to appreciate how people of various cultures have used the arts to express themselves
- The ability to understand and appreciate different artistic styles and works from representative historical periods and cultures
- Some knowledge of the social and intellectual influences affecting artistic from
- The ability to use the skills, media, tools, and processes required to express themselves in one or more of the arts

College entrants also will profit from more intensive preparations in at least one of the four areas of the arts: visual arts, theater, music, and dance.

If the preparation of college entrants is in the visual arts, they will need the following knowledge and skills:

- The ability to identify and describe—using the appropriate vocabulary—various visual art forms from different historical periods
- The ability to analyze the structure of a work of visual art
- The ability to evaluate a work of visual art
- To know how to express themselves in one or more of the visual art forms, such as drawing, painting, photography, weaving, ceramics, and sculpture

If the preparations of college entrants is in theater, they will need the following knowledge and skills:

- The ability to identify and describe—using the appropriate vocabulary—different kinds of plays from different historical periods
- The ability to analyze the structure, plot, characterization, and language of a play, both as a literary document and as a theater production
- The ability to evaluate a theater production
- To know how to express themselves by acting in a play or by improvising, or by writing a play or by directing or working behind the scenes of a theater production

If the preparation of college entrants is in music, they will need the following knowledge and skills:

- The ability to listen perceptively to music, distinguishing such elements as pitch, rhythm, timbre, and dynamics
- The ability to read music
- The ability to evaluate a musical work or performance
- To know how to express themselves by playing an instrument, singing in a group or individually, or composing music

If the preparation of college entrants is in dance, they will need the following knowledge and skills:

- The ability to identify and describe—using the appropriate vocabulary—dances of various cultures and historical periods
- The ability to analyze various techniques, styles, and choreographic forms

- The ability to evaluate a dance performance
- To know how to express themselves through dancing or choreography

Mathematics

College entrants will need the following basic mathematical proficiency:

- The ability to apply mathematical techniques in the solution of real life problems and to recognize when to apply those techniques
- Familiarity with the language, notation, and deductive nature of mathematics and the ability to express quantitative ideas with precision
- The ability to use computers and calculators
- Familiarity with the basic concepts of statistics and statistical reasoning
- Knowledge in considerable depth and detail of algebra, geometry, and functions

More specifically, college entrants will need the following preparation in mathematics:

Computing

- Familiarity with computer programming and the use of prepared computer programs in mathematics
- The ability to use mental computation and estimation to evaluate calculator and computer results
- Familiarity with the methods used to solve mathematical problems with calculators or computers as the tools

Statistics

- The ability to gather and interpret data and to represent them graphically
- The ability to apply techniques for summarizing data using such statistical concepts such as average, median, and mode

- Familiarity with techniques of statistical reasoning and common misuses of statistics

Algebra

- Skill in solving equations and inequalities
- Skill in operations with real numbers
- Skill in simplifying algebraic expressions, including simple rational and radical expressions
- Familiarity with permutations, combinations, simple counting problems, and the binomial theorem

Geometry

- Knowledge of two- and three-dimensional figures and their properties
- The ability to think of two- and three-dimensional figures in terms of symmetry, congruence, and similarity
- The ability to use the Pythagorean theorem and special right triangle relationships
- The ability to draw geometrical figures and use geometrical modes of thinking in the solving of problems

Functions

- Knowledge of relations, functions, and inverses
- The ability to graph linear and quadratic functions and use them in the interpretation and solution of problems

College entrants expecting to major in science or engineering or to take advanced courses in mathematics or computer science will need the following more extensive mathematical proficiency:

Computing

- The ability to write computer programs to solve a variety of mathematical problems
- Familiarity with the methodology of developing computer programs and with the considerations of design, structure, and style that are an important part of this methodology

Statistics

- Understanding of simulation techniques used to model experimental situations
- Knowledge of elementary concepts of probability needed in the study and understanding of statistics

Algebra

- Skill in solving trigonometric, exponential, and logarithmic equations
- Skill in operations with complex numbers
- Familiarity with arithmetic and geometric series and with proofs by mathematical induction
- Familiarity with simple matrix operations and their relation to systems of linear equations

Geometry

- Appreciation of the role of proofs and axiomatic structure in mathematics and the ability to write proofs
- Knowledge of analytic geometry in the plane
- Knowledge of the conic sections
- Familiarity with vectors and with the use of polar coordinates

Functions

- Knowledge of various types of functions, including polynomial, exponential, logarithmic, and circular functions
- The ability to graph such functions and to use them in the solution of problems

Science

College entrants will need the following preparation in science:

Laboratory and Field Work

- The ability to distinguish between scientific evidence and personal opinion by inquiry and questioning

- The ability to recognize the role of observation and experimentation in the development of scientific theories
- Sufficient familiarity with laboratory and field work to ask appropriate scientific questions and to recognize what is involved in experimental approaches to the solutions of such questions
- The skills to gather scientific information through laboratory, field, and library work
- The ability to organize and communicate the results obtained by observation and experimentation

Mathematical Skills

- A quantitative understanding of at least one field of science—an understanding that employs the basic mathematical proficiency for all students outlined in the foregoing description of learning outcomes in mathematics
- The ability to interpret data presented in tabular and graphic form
- The ability to draw conclusions and make inferences from data
- The ability to select and apply mathematical relationships to scientific problems
- The ability to use mathematical relationships to describe results obtained by observations and experimentation
- The ability to interpret, in nonmathematical language, relationships presented in mathematical form

Fundamental Concepts

Understanding in some depth the unifying concepts of the life and physical sciences, including cell theory, geological evolution, organic evolution, atomic structure, chemical bonding, and transformation of energy.

Detailed Knowledge

College entrants will need detailed knowledge of at least one field of science, usually the same field in which they have developed a quantitative understanding. This detailed knowledge could be in the earth sciences or in one of the newer, interdisciplinary fields of science.

It could also be in one of the more traditional fields: biology, chemistry, or physics.

In biology such detailed knowledge includes the central concepts, principles, and basic factual material of most, if not all, of the following topics: molecular and cellular aspects of living things, structure and function in plants and animals, genetics, evolution, plant and animal diversity and principles of classification, ecological relationships, and animal behavior.

In chemistry such detailed knowledge includes the central concepts, principles, and basic factual material of most, if not all, of the following topics: states of matter, structure of matter, solutions, reactions of matter (including acid-base and oxidation reduction), stoichiometry, energy changes in chemical reactions, equilibrium, kinetics, and descriptive chemistry (including periodic classification, metals, nonmetals, and introductory organic chemistry).

In physics such detailed knowledge includes the central concepts, principles, and basic factual material of most, if not all, of the following topics: mechanics, optics, wave phenomena, electricity and magnetism, heat and kinetic theory, atomic and nuclear physics, and relativity.

College entrants expecting to major in scientific fields will need theorem-extensive mathematical proficiency for such students outlined in the mathematics section.

Additional quantitatively based scientific study will also be important.

Social Studies

All college entrants will need the following general understanding of the social studies:

- Basic factual knowledge of major political and economic institutions and their historical development
- Basic factual knowledge of the social and cultural fields of history
- An introductory knowledge of the content and concepts of the social sciences
- A grasp of major trends in the contemporary world (for example, nationalism or urbanization)
- Familiarity with a variety of written, numerical, and visual forms of data

- Familiarity with the techniques of quantitative and nonquantitative analysis
- Familiarity with diverse interpretations of data

History

College entrants will need certain general knowledge and skills in political, social, and cultural history.

- Some understanding of the relationship between present and past, including contrasts between contemporary institutions and values and those of the past, the reasons for these contrasts, and leading continuities between past and present
- Some understanding of how to approach the problem of change over time
- The ability to recognize historical cause and effect
- The ability to identify major historical turning points
- Some ability to develop historical interpretations

More specifically, college entrants will need the following basic knowledge:

United States History

- The chronology and impact of political events, development of governmental and other social institutions, technological and environmental changes, and changes in social and cultural values
- The interaction among people of different national origins, races, and cultures, and how such interaction has shaped American history
- The relationship between events and historical trends in the United States and trends elsewhere in the world, developed through analysis of major similarities and differences

World Geography and Culture

- The basic features of major societies and cultures in the contemporary world: their geography, major economic and social structures, political systems, and religions
- The international context of contemporary diplomacy and economics

- The historical developments underlying present connections and similarities among the world's peoples, and the major differences dividing them
- The chronology and significance of major events and movements in world history (for example, the Renaissance, the Industrial Revolution, and the spread of Islam)

Social Science

College entrants will need the following basic knowledge and skills in the social sciences:

- The ability to understand the basic information developed by the social sciences, including statistical data and other materials
- Familiarity with the basic method of the social sciences, that is, with the framing and empirical testing of hypotheses
- A basic understanding of at least one of the social sciences (for example, economics, political science, geography, or sociology) and of how its practitioners define and solve problems
- Familiarity with how to approach a social topic or institution by means of ideas drawn from several social sciences

Foreign Language

College entrants will need proficiency in another language and culture that provides the following skills:

- The ability to ask and answer questions and maintain a simple conversation in areas of immediate need or on very familiar topics
- The ability to pronounce the language well enough to be intelligible to native speakers
- The ability to understand, with some repetition, simple questions and statements
- The ability to read and understand the information presented in a simple paragraph
- The ability to write a short paragraph on a familiar topic

- The ability to deal with some everyday situations in the culture such as greetings, leave-takings, buying food, and asking directions

Students with this basic proficiency will also need some knowledge of the culture, history, and life patterns of the society or societies in which the language is spoken.

College entrants who expect to follow an advanced program of study in another language or in other subjects requiring language skills will need greater proficiency. It will provide the following skills:

- The ability to engage in conversation about such subjects as school activities, personal interests, and autobiographical information
- The ability to understand the essential points of a lecture, narrative, or explanation delivered at moderate speed
- The ability to read and comprehend some literature and most factual information in nontechnical prose such as newspaper articles addressed to the general reader
- The ability to write several paragraphs of reasonably coherent and correct prose to produce summaries, descriptions of events, or social correspondence
- The ability to handle routine social situations in a culturally correct manner showing understanding of common rules of how individuals behave toward one another

Students with this greater proficiency also will need some knowledge of the history, geography, institutions, current political situation, and the intellectual and artistic achievements of the society or societies in which the language is spoken.

Learning outcomes in a classical language take a different form, since Latin and ancient Greek are generally taught not as spoken languages but as literary languages. Thus, the two principal outcomes are reading comprehension and some knowledge of Roman or Greek culture. The proficiency expected of college entrants whose language preparation is in Latin or Greek is reflected in the following skills:

- The ability to understand reading materials of low difficulty, that is, adapted or simplified texts

- The ability to give a reasonably accurate account of the contents of the reading material by answering questions, paraphrasing, or summarizing

Students intending to undertake advanced study in a classical language will need, in addition, the following skills:

- The ability to understand authentic unsimplified prose or poetry without undue reliance on a dictionary
- The ability to translate prose or poetry into reasonably accurate English

The College Board's (1983) outline of the basic academic subjects is a practical, manageable place to start with what to teach. You will find this outline the basis for sample lesson plans in the Resources section. Refer to this list to remind you of your most basic academic goals. When you plan any classroom activity, you should be able to justify it on the basis of this outline. You should find it helpful if you have to give a rationale for your lesson plans to a parent, department chair, or school administrator. Refer to this outline often!

Using the Range of Teaching Strategies and Media

I'd rather learn from one bird how to sing than teach ten thousand stars how not to dance.
(e.e. cummings in Eisner, 1979, p. 261)

This section begins by identifying the variety of teaching strategies available and outlining how in a given school year a teacher could easily diversify instruction to the benefit of all students. It also includes a discussion of the methods and the advantages of small group work as a staple of teaching. With the exception of the description of using small groups, I do not try to explicate techniques for the other strategies in detail. One reason for this is that I think you will have enough familiarity with the methods you are willing to try. Another reason is that to cover them in-depth is reason for a separate book like one of the recommended books by Anthony Jones (Jones, Bagford, & Wallen, 1979) or Bruce Joyce (1992). Finally, the procedures will be dictated more by the classroom activity itself than by any conventional approach to recognized teaching strategies.

Strategies

When I began my first year of teaching, I was badly unprepared for the demands of finding enough meaningful activities for my students to last the entire year. If it hadn't been for Scholastic's *Scope Magazine,* I honestly don't know what I would have done. Having taught for over 30 years now, I never have enough time to do all I want to do. I thought it might be helpful to think about the list of all the different strategies for teaching available and then share my experience with how easy it is to have 180 different classroom activities for a school year and how I think those activities might be paced.

There are so many teaching strategies. The challenge is to continue to add to your repertoire. There's an understandable tendency to stick with what you are most familiar with. Boring! Commit yourself to trying something different regularly. I admit I was uncomfortable with role-playing at first, but it became one of my favorite teaching techniques. One of my greatest frustrations is to see teachers limit themselves to one or two techniques associated with their subject matter: the math teacher who overrelies on the overhead, the history teacher who relies on lecture, the English teacher who relies on large group discussions. You may have a favorite method you use most often, but for goodness sake, use a variety of methods.

For help with developing additional strategies I recommend Anthony Jones's *Strategies for Teaching* and Bruce Joyce's (1992) *Models of Teaching*. I am confident that somewhere in your time in school you have experienced the case study, contract learning, demonstrations, inquiry, discussion—large groups, discussion—small groups, drill, field trips, guided imagery, independent study, interviews, lab experiences, learning centers, learning packets, lecture, observation, problem solving, projects, questioning, role-playing, simulations, Socratic dialogue, student presentations, tests, trials, and tutorials.

I list these strategies to emphasize the wide variety of methods available to you. Similarly, I am confident you have also seen a wide variety of media put to good use, including books, bulletin boards, cassettes, CDs, chalkboards, charts, film clips, graphs, guests, handouts, magazines, newspapers, overheads, pictures, and slides. The more real the classroom experience, generally the better. I annotate this list in the hope of getting you to think how you could use each of these media to diversify your own teaching.

Some Brief Annotations on Media

Books. Partial sets from the school bookroom can be used for group work; find a resource such as the public library that sells books for under $1.00; you can justify tearing a book that costs a dollar or less into its segments, and get a good class out of individual students reading different parts and summarizing what they read to the entire class.

Bulletin boards. "Heroes" related to your subject and chosen by the class are good topics.

Cassettes and CDs. Students can often find course themes in the music they are listening to.

Chalkboards. Try to put up your outlines before the students arrive.

Charts. Charts tend to be boring, but students need to learn to read them.

Film clips. Watch out for inappropriate language, but film clips are second only to real life for experiences by which to master concepts.

Graphs. Graphs tend to be boring, but students need to learn to read them.

Guests. Most guests can't hold student attention unless you handle the guest like a talk show host would—keep discussion moving.

Handouts. I love handouts, if your photocopy budget will allow it. They tend to keep the student on-task, and if they are last-minute copies, copyright restrictions probably do not apply.

Magazines. Magazines tend to be expensive and difficult for obtaining class sets (but I love Scholastic's publications, especially *Scope Magazine*).

Newspapers. Newspapers are a good way to get your students reading, and most local newspapers have very inexpensive programs for classroom sets.

Overheads. Overheads can work if you don't overuse them (math teachers especially tend to overrely on overheads).

Pictures. Pictures can be effective, but are often too small for the entire class to see from their desks and tend not to be as effective as video clips.

Slides. Slides too often tend to be boring.

The experienced teacher is always on the lookout for class sets of anything he or she might use. I recently picked up 35 free copies of the Declaration of Independence. No immediate use, but I now have them on hand!

As far as teaching strategies go, I add the following comments.

The case study. Find some good ones and hang on to them; this can be a great device if it is well selected. I have one with clues taken anonymously from a student's school cumulative file that I often use.

Contract learning. This is too time-consuming to use with most students, but a life saver for the student in trouble or who can't get to school for some reason such as illness.

Demonstrations. I like to do oral interpretations of literature. Students humor me. Often they have excellent skills they might show off as well.

Inquiry. The open-ended quality of inquiry makes some teachers nervous, but a "discovery" can make it worthwhile.

Discussion—large group. This is a pervasive teaching technique, but I know of no one who can consistently keep an entire class involved for very long.

Discussion—small group. I love structured questionnaires for students to discuss in small groups; this gets many students involved.

Drill. My student teachers are sometimes surprised to find out how much I like drills, because they aren't thought of as being very creative. In small, frequent doses stressing only the most basic course material, drills can be very worthwhile.

Field trips. One day our school had three field trips. On the first trip, two students disappeared. On the second, a student climbed into the zoo's alligator pit. On the third, a student had a fist fight with the bus driver. Field trips take a lot of planning for what are often limited pay offs.

Guided imagery. This can help students get over mental blocks about your subject; it is excellent in skill areas for helping students picture success.

Independent study. Most of us rarely live up to our expectations for follow-through, but such an approach can help certain students.

Interviews. Interviews are much better than guest speakers because you can help keep the presentation moving and interesting by inserting timely questions.

Lab experience. Labs have to be well conceived, with particular attention to time limits.

Learning centers. I love learning centers, but they are difficult to do with older students.

Learning packets. I rarely use them, but they are great for chores such as grammar.

Lecture. Lectures are poor for student retention and are mostly used for authoritarian control of the class, but I like short, mini, power lectures where the students know they will be short and on the test.

Observation. Make something happen and have the students tell or write what they see—the "enlightened eye" is a key to all good education.

Problem solving. This is particularly good for real classroom issues and problems.

Projects. Figuring out how to grade them is the problem. Otherwise, students usually like to do them.

Questioning. I love to take a student and an issue and probe as long and as deep as we can both stand it. Also, having students learn to ask good questions is imperative.

Role-playing. I like role-playing, but it is not an easy technique to master. More than any other of these techniques, this one needs someone to show you how to do it.

Simulations. I've done them. They have worked well. I'd generally advise to try this technique after you've mastered most of the others. It is complex, and if one part falls apart, the entire thing fails.

Socratic dialogue. This is one of my best and favorite techniques, but it isn't easy and is impossible to do with large groups. Also, the discussants must start with good comprehension of the text you are discussing. If you want to get into this, The Great Books Foundation in Chicago has a Web site (http://www.greatbooks.org) and excellent 2-day training sessions throughout the United States.

Student presentations. Set a time limit, perhaps 5 minutes, and this can go well. But generally, students are not accomplished presenters, so keep presentations short and successful.

Tests. Don't overtest, but have excellent cumulative exams that test the most important course material.

Trials. I have come to prefer "hearings." Whether it is history, literature, or current events, I assign each student a different role (and thus source of knowledge), take everyone's testimony, and have a jury decide.

Tutorials. These are time-consuming. Use other students to do them as you can, and be patient when you do choose to do one.

The key is to diversify instruction. It will tend to get everyone more involved overall. Variety is the spice of life. And it will keep you fresh.

180 Activities for a School Year

Although I discuss the issues of organization and pacing the curriculum in the next section, I want to demonstrate how easy it is to diversify your teaching strategies.

A school year has approximately 180 school days scattered over 10 months. If you use, for example, the read-along activity just once a month, that would account for 10 of the 180 lessons. *All this list is trying to establish is that there are a lot of alternative teaching strategies and one need not be overly dependent on any one approach.* Appreciate differences, diversify instruction. Variety is the spice of life. Naturally, you should be equally conscientious in ensuring that the variety is used to teach only the most important aspects of your curriculum.

Planning Lessons and Teaching Strategies 47

(Please note that 10 of one activity would be only once a month for that activity, which I note to suggest, once again, how easy it is to diversify your curriculum.)

Total Number of Days in Year	Activity
1-10	Reviews, lectures, large group discussions
11-20	Tests (at least 50% of tests on higher levels of cognition: concepts, skills, analysis; at least 60% of tests on what every student should have learned)
21-30	Films/videotapes
31-40	Assignments in class set of newspapers (fosters critical thinking and life-long learning)
41-50	A trial or hearing; haiku (see Resources); 25 words (see Resources); field trips (one a semester); students write exam; other Resources activities
51-60	Read-along activities (teacher reads text aloud; students alternate unrehearsed reading; read out loud alternately in small groups; students read material into audio tape)
61-65	Videotape student presentations and play them to class
66-70	Teach study skills for your subject
71-80	Guest speakers
81-100	Student presentations
101-105	Assignments in library
106-110	Role-playing (e.g., Chelser, 1966)
111-120	Have students write observations of some picture, incident, article, or the like pertaining to your subject
121-140	Use small groups
141-145	Dyads (see Resources)
146-150	Time in class to work on projects
151-160	Case studies of problems in your subject area
161-165	Ill/assemblies/catch-up work
166-170	Show off your best stuff as a teacher
171-175	Tear up a book or magazine into sections and have students summarize their parts in full class (see Resources)
176-180	Other activities from the Resources section

Figure 2.3. Diversity is the spice of life.

Commentary on the Activities for a School Year

I consider using small groups the staple of teaching strategies (Gose, 1989). I quickly came to this conclusion my first semester of teaching because I was not as effective as I wanted to be with either lecture or full class discussions. It is not only because I do not do lectures or large group discussions well that I am so critical of these methods. I have known only one high school teacher in my 30-year teaching career who I thought consistently used lecture effectively and exceptionally. He was a history teacher and a great raconteur. Overwhelmingly, I argue that the textbook, not the lecture, is the best place to cover content. Students can read two or three times faster than the teacher can talk, can go back over passages, and can find the material in an attractive format. This does not mean that I never use lecture. I like "power lectures," concentrated lectures that cover vital material and where the students are told exactly how long the lecture will be so that they can fully concentrate.

I do not, for the most part, like full class discussions because too many students are unable to participate in the conversation, too many will not be paying attention, it too easily degenerates into mere opinion giving (instead of analysis or informed opinion giving), and far too often a student will feel alienated for not having been called on. I am much more likely to give a power lecture than to try to lead a full class discussion for 30 students.

Besides, research from scholars such as Leslie Hart (1978) finds that we learn by talking. With small groups (and dyads—see Resources), students can learn more by talking more, if you direct suitably.

I suggest in the list of activities for the 180-day school year a wide variety of teaching strategies and with it the oft-mentioned "appreciate differences, diversify instruction." Most of the strategies will be familiar and easily implemented. Each strategy has its own set-up needs. Sell the power lecture as important for the exams and do not overuse it. I recommend film clips instead of full films for the most part. Students too often think of films as sleep time. Make sure students clearly know why they are seeing the film clips. After each clip, clarify the issues and ask for questions. I call this "commentary" instead of lecture or full class discussion because the comments are much briefer than a lecture would be in clarifying the film experience, and the class questions should be handled efficiently prior to proceeding with the next film clip instead of being the occasion for a sustained full class discussion.

If you are tearing up a book into parts for each student to read and summarize their respective part, you should be very careful about emphasizing your respect for books and that this particular lesson justifies this use of a book because of the relevance of the content and the students' need to be able to read, summarize, and explain aloud, as well as to learn from each other. Whatever teaching device or strategy you use, it needs to be "sold" (see the section on motivation) and set up. You can lose a class for the rest of the period because of poor transitions, failing to check whether your equipment works, or forgetting part of the lesson at home on your kitchen table.

You probably have sufficient experience as a student to try most of the techniques identified. Books like Bruce Joyce's (1992) *Models of Teaching* can help you develop more sophisticated strategies later. I offer the following more detailed description of working with small groups, however, as a staple of teaching, the staple of my own game plan. The sensitive reader may notice an uncanny parallel with this staple of teaching and the principle discussed in the section on discipline—divide and conquer. Ha. Running a well-conceived curriculum does tend to create effective discipline.

Using Small Group Discussions[2]

There's nothing magic about small group discussions. Used improperly, they can be just as tedious as poor lectures and poorly directed large group discussions. But when they are led effectively, they have several virtues.

They are well-suited for learning higher-order teaching skills. In terms of Bloom's taxonomy, discussions are much more suitable for the upper levels of cognition, including application, analysis, synthesis, and evaluation, than are lectures.

Small group discussions are also well-suited for allowing students to practice the communication and social skills that are so requisite for "success" in and out of school.

Small group discussions allow more students more time to "learn by talking." In the large group format, only one student can "learn" this way at one time. But with the use of small groups, many students can be learning by talking simultaneously without interfering with each other. If you have several groups of five students in a small group, each student could average 10 minutes of talking in a 50-minute period, as compared to less than 2 minutes each in the large group discussion format. This gives each student significantly more time to "internalize content" by having to explain it to someone else. Students also learn more by more talking, by putting ideas into new, and often more complicated, relationships with each other.

Further, small group discussions make it easier for the teacher to enjoy him/herself. Instead of the pressure of being in front of the class lecturing, or at the hub of the communication network leading a large group discussion, the teacher can move about freely within the class, not only monitoring students' progress, but listening, adding comments, sharing, relaxing, appreciating students, instead of being "under the gun" as is so often true when one is the focal point of attention.

As indicated earlier, these virtues exist only if the small group discussion is well conceived. After having used small group discussions extensively, I have identified a number of essentials for the success of small group discussions.

I have found that the most important consideration, by far, is the choice of topics and the questions on that topic. The research review by Gage and Berliner (1979) indicates that "low-consensus" (thus prospectively controversial) subjects generally promote more discussion than "high-consensus" topics. That low consensus has to be among the actual group members, not just low consensus in the society at large. There may be controversy in our society over bussing, but if no one in your small group has experienced the consequences of bussing either directly or indirectly, there's not likely to be a lot of discussion or debate. The topic of discussion must, therefore, tie, somehow directly, into the students' motivation. If the students are told that questions to be discussed are going to reappear on a later exam, even a high-consensus topic might be effective. The discussion's relationship to a future test is only one way of motivating students to consider your questions seriously. Certainly, the topics and questions will be enhanced if they create surprise, arouse curiosity, are relevant to some current issue facing people in the class, whet the appetite for future experiences, require what has previously been learned, or relate to students' interests.

Another criteria I often used to decide whether the topic and questions are likely to work is how they will likely affect a student personally. As often as possible, questions should require students to relate your subject's content to either personal experience or personal opinion. One of my small groups included a discussion about the short story "The Public Hating," by Steve Allen. The story has numerous parallels to Shirley Jackson's more familiar story, "The Lottery." In the story, a person found guilty of treason is led into Yankee Stadium and killed by the collective hate of the 65,000 in attendance. The questions given us to discuss were excellent, but even more fascinating was the revelation by one of our group members that she had actually seen an execution. The story, coupled with this person's experience, led to an earnest consideration by our group of the effects of capital punishment. You certainly cannot plan on your questions eliciting such dramatic parallels in personal experience. But you should be able to anticipate what many of your students will find interesting. And knowing whether your topic will "work" with your students requires the wisdom and knowledge of your particular group of students that only you have. I have found that thinking about the topic at the same time I am thinking, at least in the back of my mind, about my students and thinking about both over a long period of time, is as valuable as an hour or two of hard work on the topic for my small group discussion. A great topic, however, is not sufficient in and of itself. Even with a great topic, you will have a number of other administrative choices to make.

You will have to make some difficult choices about the size and membership of your small groups. In his writing teams, Dan Fader (1976) has found three-person groups a good size. Elizabeth Cohen (n.d.) has often used four in her experimental groups. Five-person groups are especially effective in group projects that require multiple skills and resources a smaller group might not have access to. I generally don't like to use groups larger than five persons, but, as one of my student teachers pointed out, too many groups in a classroom can become a problem to monitor. Perhaps groups can be effective with as many as seven members. As always, and as with any educational decision, there are tradeoffs and no prescriptions or absolutes. The toughest choice about group membership is whether to let friends be with friends. If friends are together and "into" the topic, the results can be wonderful. Conversely, groups of friends are probably more likely to abandon the topic more quickly and socialize if things drag at all. You can make students in the same "rows as a group," or count (1, 2, 3, 4; 1, 2, 3, 4; etc., with the 1s together, 2s together, etc.). You can point to certain students and group them in an area of the room. You can put students together with the same zodiac signs, or middle initials, or names alphabetically spelled backward. If you use a variety of selections, you can let friends be together sometimes but with everyone else in the class at some other time. It's certainly fair to try to avoid problems when making your assignments (e.g., by not putting an ex-boyfriend and girlfriend together the day they break up). I have even been known to tell a class I want six groups of five in less than 90 seconds; an experienced class can accomplish that goal without anyone feeling left out.

In some instances, it is helpful to assign (or ask students to appoint) students to certain roles in each group. A secretary to keep written track of the group answers to the questions is often helpful. Sometimes, a group spokesperson can be appointed to report the group's answers back to the large group. Sometimes, but not always, you might assign one student to lead the discussion. Sometimes, you might appoint one person to make sure everyone receives an equal opportunity to participate. Because of the importance of the "independence of the peer group" for students to practice independent group skills, and after having gotten my students used to the small group discussions format, I usually prefer the roles to emerge from within the group.

Choose your topic, appoint your groups, decide about roles, and then give each group a handout of the questions you want discussed. Most students from kindergarten to graduate school need something in their hands to focus their attention on. Usually, some activity will have preceded the small group discussion, whether a lecture, movie, reading assignment, event, or guest speaker. But in most circumstances, the group will still need help in focusing its discussion. You can also ask the group members to generate their own questions about the topic. Even then, you will want to hand out sample questions to the group. (My experience is that one, and only one, copy of these questions per group helps focus all the individuals on the common task.) Such a handout not only helps focus attention, but also enhances the credibility, and then your "P. R.," with the class. Also, by needing only five or six copies of your questions per class, you can handwrite your questions and use carbon paper, which has the benefit of not requiring you to have access to a photocopying or ditto machine that may not be readily available.

Once you have chosen a great topic, divided up your groups, assigned (or not assigned) roles, and given each group a handout, don't bog yourself down justifying the topic or giving a lot of directions. You've already sold them on the idea that discussions yield higher-order objectives; permit students a chance to practice vital social skills; give them all a greater opportunity to learn by talking; and add a bit more enjoyment to their day. Now don't let them hook you with distractions. Ninety-nine percent of students will immediately figure out what to do. You are going to have to talk to the 1% that didn't figure it out personally anyway. Get them started promptly.

While you don't want to bog students down with directions, you do need them to be accountable. I have used at least three formats to ensure accountability: 1) A scribe can write down the group's "answers" to the questions to turn in at the end of class; 2) A spokesperson can briefly report major conclusions to the larger class at the end of the session; and 3) If you have enough tape recorders, you can have each group tape its discussion (which you can review on the tape player in your car on your commute to or from school). Each of these methods has its advantages and disadvantages. All increase the credibility of the assignment, that is, you are serious and the discussion is important.

Having gotten students into their small groups, you want to monitor them. You will find it magical how every time you walk into a group's social space, the on-task talk will increase. Do a good bit of circulating. While moving from group to group, you can clarify, cajole, badger, advise, insert, spin, fold, and mutilate as you see fit to keep the groups happy and making progress with the questions. You can also assure them that certain digressions are permissible. Enjoy yourself; enjoy your students. You certainly didn't enter teaching for the money or hassle-free days. Plan to have a great time.

As you monitor, you will probably start worrying about what to do with the groups that are going to finish well ahead of the others. You have already prepared for that eventuality by making the last question or two more open-ended, but less necessary, to cover the scheduled time. This does not penalize the slow groups for not finishing. You can slow the fast group down by sitting in with it and prolonging a question or two. You can ask the group that finishes first to write one or two more related questions that you might use next time you use this assignment. In a pinch, I keep a bottom drawer of mazes and other puzzles that I may hand out without comment to members who finish early. ("No, I didn't say you had to do it. I thought you might like a way to work on your other thinking processes instead of wasting your time.")

When everyone is finished, how do you grade them? You can't realistically make a qualitative judgment. To give letter grades on the basis of what the secretary writes down, the spokesperson reports, or you hear on tapes invites a host of problems. If you do give a grade, I advise giving everyone the same number of participation points for successful completion of the task. This allows you to use a threat you hope you won't have to make—"Do you want a zero for the day?"—without having to worry about As, Bs, Cs, Ds, and Fs.

At the end of the small group discussion, you may want to hear a spokesperson report major findings to the class. If you do, make these brief. Your students will not easily make the transition from the free flow of their small group discussion to the inherent restraints of the large group discussion. After they have had their brief say, it is most appropriate for you to offer the summation. You can put all the points of view into some kind of perspective, probably a perspective that relates to your subject matter. You should be able to do this in 3 to 5 minutes. The music teacher might relate the discussion to musical genres; the history teacher to methods of research; the English teacher to the elements of the short story (plot, theme, character, setting, point of view). This summation is important because it reminds the students the assignment has serious educational intent and their discussion is relevant (somehow) to the course objectives.

I have had a lot of success using small group discussions and at least ostensibly following these recommendations. That does not mean the process evolves like a well-rehearsed play. Sometimes there's a bit of confusion; sometimes students don't stay on the topics; sometimes it's a bit noisy. So what? If you've chosen a good topic and asked good questions, you should incite some confusion, digressions, and noise. Besides, isn't the socialization process at least half of what schooling is about anyway? And did you think they were all really listening to the lecture or large group discussion anyway? Of course not. At least here, you have some behavioral indications of lapses in attention that you can adjust and respond to. To my mind, that's quite unlike, but preferable, to the false and misleading performances inattentive students have managed in making it look like they are paying attention to lectures and large group discussions when they are not. Small group discussion can be one of the most enjoyable staples in the repertoire of teaching techniques.

Organization and Pacing the Curriculum

Unlike skill-based teachers, who are dominated by routines and set ways of assessing, contracting, and completing tasks, creative teachers are more willing to vary the rhythm, pace, and tempo of their lessons.

(Barrie Barrell)

This section consists of five separate but related parts. The first part is my recommendations about the ABCs of teaching. In this part, I strongly recommend planning each class with at least three prospective activities in mind: an introductory activity to settle students into the class period; a major activity covering the required curriculum; and a highly interesting third activity if your second activity finishes (or dies) early. This is by far the most important section for the beginning teacher. You must be able to get successfully through each class period. If you can find meaningful ABC activities for each period, you will have a level of success. It will take awhile before you can consistently plan three such activities per class period. This is the place to start, the place that will ensure survival and some success.

The subsequent sections alert you to larger issues in planning. The second part is "My Student Teachers Don't Do Lesson Plans," a review of how experienced teachers plan. The third part includes notes and hints about pacing for the individual teacher and notes about varying the class activities over the week and term. The fourth part characterizes identifiable parameters that influence the pacing and rhythm of the school day, week, month, term, and year. The fifth part offers comments on lesson plans. Prototypical, "instant" lesson plans for most subject areas are included in the Resources section.

The ABCs of Teaching

In all my years as a professional educator, I have been critical of formal lesson plans. I have also been acutely sensitive about my own bias that each teacher has to learn to teach his or her own way. After successfully teaching high school, I had an opportunity to teach fourth grade. I replaced a very popular teacher and had the "misfortune" to observe him the week before I took over the class. I tried to use his material and approach. I should have known better. His material and approach did not work for me. I had to do and accept what would work for me. Now that I am in teacher education, I am determined not to be prescriptive. Emerson (1967) warns that imitation is suicide and that "we are diminished by anyone who falls under our banner" (p. 8). I am proud of my own work as a teacher, but one of the few conceits I do not have is that anyone else should teach like I teach. I think you will be happiest if you find your own way.

After three decades in teaching, I have concluded that I need to be more straightforward in my recommendations. First, I do not like formal lesson plans. I strongly believe in being well prepared! But I never found the time-consuming writing of extensive, detailed lesson plans helpful. In fact, the time spent on them tended to take away from effective planning, and when they were too detailed, I was not sufficiently flexible to respond to unanticipated class needs and moods. They tended to take time away from really thinking through what my lessons were all about. Somewhere along the way, you should, if required, be able to identify your objectives, your rationale for your selection and organization of activities, and your means of evaluation. But I'd personally go nuts doing it all the time in great detail. Again, I believe in being prepared. Every period should have meaningful learning activities for students. But if you can think of three meaningful activities for each period, you will be way ahead of the game.

In a traditional secondary classroom, you will probably need more than one activity per period. I have found I think in terms of an A, B, and C activity. The A activity is a short activity that begins when, or shortly after, students enter the class. It helps get them into a "studious" frame of mind and gives you time to take roll and handle other classroom business. The sample A activities in the Resources are useable in a wide variety of classroom situations and are designed to help students get into a thoughtful frame of mind. They are not guaranteed to succeed. These activities have worked for me, however, partially because I have believed they will work, and they should be suggestive of the kind of activities for which you should look.

The B activities are what you can build the major lesson around. They might not take up a full classroom period, but they qualify as the period's major curricular activity. The sample B activities in the Resources are ones that might be used in a variety of classrooms. One assumption I make is that basic academic and communication skills are every teacher's business. Most teachers can adapt these activities to their own subject matter. The activities all tend to promote important skills, but they should not be perceived as substitutes for covering particular subject matter. Your major responsibility each day is to make a meaningful aspect of your overall curriculum as real as possible.

The C activities are designed for use if your other plans come up short. If you have 1 to 25 minutes left in the period, students deserve the opportunity to engage in something worthwhile and interesting. The C activities have a "game" quality about them. I would use them if only for their motivational value. But I think we also have an obligation (and to tell our students we have such an obligation) to help students think in creative, nonstandard ways to develop a flexible cognitive style. The sample C activities in the Resources are meant to be useable across a wide variety of classes and to be suggestive of the type of activities you should look for to end classes effectively.

Although the following pages will alert you to issues that affect all your curriculum planning and issues to be taken seriously, the place to start is proving to yourself and your class that you can make the individual period work successfully. Well-selected A, B, and C activities assure that level of success. If you have at hand short activities to start a class effectively, a meaningful major activity for each day, and some plans for what to do if your major lesson ends early, you have an excellent start in your teaching. The next section explains how the research evidence tends to support my ideas about successful planning.

My Student Teachers Don't Do Lesson Plans

You will probably not be surprised to find that teachers virtually never use formal lesson plans, and more often than not concentrate first on what activity they want to use.

The teachers who teach students are enjoying their careers. Those who focus only on teaching their subject matter are probably struggling. Teachers who accept the realities of the school year are managing better than those who think they can defy those gravities.

My student teachers do not do lesson plans; they are much too busy planning lessons. My failure to require lesson plans does not necessarily mean that I am an anarchist or a disestablishmentarianist. In fact I still assign Ralph Tyler's (1950) *Basic Principles of Curriculum and Instruction* (while mentioning that in a visit to our college, Tyler answered the question about his infamous four questions by saying that if he could add a fifth, he would add a question about motivation). I even introduce my own students to at least seven different lesson plan formats. However, we have had reason to know that lesson plans per se are probably not the best way to plan lessons, at least since Wittrock's (1985) *Handbook of Research on Teaching*.

In his review of the research on teacher planning as it is actually done in the profession, Wittrock (1985) concludes "that substantial teacher energy is devoted to structuring, organizing for, and managing limited classroom instructional time" (p. 260). My experience as a public school teacher and administrator substantiates that finding. My personal experience also substantiates Wittrock's conclusion that "lesson planning is rarely claimed as an important part of the repertoire of experienced teachers" (p. 260). I admit that that conclusion surprised me (perhaps more because I was surprised teachers would admit this than that it is true). From my perspective, Wittrock's review of the research validates much of any wisdom I have tried to acquire over my three decades as a teacher. Practices acquired through years of professional experience certainly deserve to be treated seriously. Wittrock finds that unit planning is the type of planning most mentioned by teachers; that written plans are sketchy, but do reflect larger planning structures and an "activity flow" (p. 260). Wittrock concludes that long-range planning is counterproductive because of interruptions during the school year, that most planning is done mentally but not on paper, that lesson plans are abandoned when the activity flow is threatened with disruption, that the activity is the basic unit for planning. Would it not be wise to prepare new teachers to do the kind of planning that experienced teachers actually do?

Wittrock (1985) also includes a review of Zahorik's judgment "that teachers who had been given plans in advance exhibited less honest or authentic use of the pupils' ideas during the lesson" and that lesson plans typically "resulted in insensitivity to pupils on the part of the teacher" (p. 267). Tending to find myself as one of those overly conscientious persons whom James Herndon (1968) satirizes with his notion of "the way it spozed to be," I remember that early in my career I was often baffled that my lessons that were a bit unbaked often went so much better that those that I had wired (to mix metaphors to suggest my befuddlement). (And I was so good at writing lesson plans for teacher education courses. . . . Nostalgically, I remember that I was particularly fond of the galvanic skin device as a way of measuring student reaction. . . .)

Naturally, it seems a lot more difficult to help beginning teachers work with the ambiguities suggested by Wittrock (1985). Are there new, more complex formulae for daily, weekly, unit, term, and yearly planning? Are there ways of writing down even the sketchy plans representative of experienced teachers that are helpful? Are there ways of planning flexibility so that the planned activities can flow more smoothly? Should we give up the joy of writing lesson plans just because they aren't particularly helpful? How can planning be used to ensure authenticity in the classroom?

I have found the ideas of F. M. Connelly (1985) from *Teachers as Curriculum Planners* very helpful in conceptualizing and planning lessons for effective instruction. Presumably influenced by Dewey, Connelly sees curriculum as experience. Because experience is never static, curriculum planning must consider the "dynamic interaction among persons, things, and processes" (p. 168). Because the curriculum is an "interaction among persons, things, and processes" (p. 168), he sees that any classroom activity has potential that can pull in different directions. This conception of curriculum resonates with Wittrock's (1985) finding that teachers emphasize activities in their planning. Because of the interactive dimension of the curriculum, Connelly emphasizes cycles and rhythms. Connelly finds that though beginning teachers can do lesson plans, "it is in the teaching that they often experience difficulty" (p. 168). Connelly argues that "rhythmic knowledge of teaching" (p. 168) is critical for success, and that experienced teachers

> know the downtimes will be followed by uptimes; they know that cyclic disruptions are temporary; they know that the end of a cycle, whether it is day's end, week's end, or year's end, is characterized by special features and that activities will be experienced differently at these times. (p. 168)

Beginning teachers, of course, do not yet have direct experience of these cycles. Nonetheless, Connelly (1985) concludes that

> the first years of teaching are crucial to becoming a teacher for it is in those first years that a teacher develops his or her rhythmic sense of knowing the classroom and of knowing how to teach. (p. 168)

I believe this to be true, and that standardized lesson plans per se are likely to be counterproductive to the learning of these rhythms. Yet believing in the paramount importance of planning lessons, in being organized, how can novice teachers be helped to develop the kind of skills necessary for successful curriculum planning?

This makes me nervous. After 30 years in the profession and in refusing to be prescriptive in any way, I have finally come to admit that "recipes" can be helpful (and, yes, I am deliberately mixing metaphors again to suggest a degree of continuing befuddlement). I've changed my mind about recipes because of the gourmet cooking classes I have taken over the past 2 years. Just this past summer, I finally got to the point where I don't necessarily need any recipes to fix up a worthy concoction in the kitchen all by myself. (An essential point in this regard is to know what goes together and to take advantage of the best and freshest ingredients at hand—which I think has obvious implications for planning curriculum.) Although I started with a slavish adherence to the recipes, I gradually found that I could vary proportions and even substitute ingredients on the basis of both previous experience and intuition. Although I have historically resisted recipes in curriculum development (among other reasons because I was fearful they would hinder my own development as a true curriculum artiste), I am now admitting that they might be helpful, as long as they are flexible enough for the teacher to adapt readily.

Experienced teachers know about the highs at the beginning of a school year, the lows near Christmas, the rise with the New Year, and the descent after June 1st. I suspect that one can warn new teachers about those ups and downs, but that such knowledge will not be helpful to teachers trying to find their more basic cycles and rhythms. I have found that beginning teachers can readily come to appreciate the rhythms of a school week, and thinking in terms of at least a week helps beginning teachers to avoid the stasis that comes with focusing planning on the individual lesson per se. Certainly there are idiosyncratic qualities to a teacher's week, but I think there are certain tendencies.

Anticipating that there will be a Monday in a school week, and more and more school holidays are now taken on Monday instead of Friday, the Monday is usually the day students are most sedate (a relative term). They have for the most part slept in later on Saturday and Sunday, so at least for the morning classes they may not be fully awake. This is often the day that will be the best for the more formal presentation of subject matter. This might include lectures, guest speakers, formal student presentations, and review of the text. If students are ever going to take notes in class (other than the day before an exam), this is likely to be the day.

Unless the teacher's goal is to keep the students as passive as possible, Tuesday is a day for the pendulum to swing from the listening/watching mode to something that involves the student in an immediate and involving activity with as little teacher command of student attention as possible. This is an excellent time for small group work. Assuming that Leslie Hart (1978) is correct in his findings that students learn by talking, this is a day in which students should talk to each other. If Monday is the day in which the teacher's performance has the best chance of success, Tuesday is the day students are most likely to make a serious contribution.

Wednesdays are often known as the "hump day." This is the middle day of the week, the day to get over. Having assured students of your serious academic intent on Monday, having reassured them on Tuesday that they can make meaningful contributions, Wednesday is often a time for seat work reading assignments, writing assignments, and even read-arounds. The teacher still has to sell the lesson, but the reading or writing assignment should have a better chance of working than expecting them either to pay attention or to become involved when students are wondering why it was that on Sunday they were ready to go back to school.

Most good teachers prefer to test on Thursdays. Friday tests are usually for discipline problems, because the restlessness that comes with Fridays is often the day for the most behavioral problems. Tests are still seen as big events in school. Testing earlier in the week than Thursday may make for too many days of letdown after the pressure of an exam. On Thursdays, students are still able to focus their attention on the subject at hand. I have found students usually do their best exam work on this day, and what teacher would not want that? Thursdays are also better days for full attendance (and avoiding as much as possible the problems of make-up work). It is the best day to bear down before the end of the week and to ask for the best academic effort the students are likely to produce.

Fridays are generally the most chaotic day of the week. School activities are most often scheduled on this day, whether athletic events, plays, or musical performances. By the end of the day, the athletes, cheerleaders, and band members are probably going to have permission to leave class. And even though an exam might help discipline that day, if the exam does not last the entire period, the teacher is inviting chaos. Because this is the day to expect the most absences, it is probably not a good idea to have an assignment that is critical for success in the entire course. If you have general control of the classroom, this is often the day for the most intrinsically rewarding lesson, the lesson with the most pizzazz, the most stimulating, involving innovative, interactive lessons.

I am quite aware that these comments about the days of the week reflect my limited and personal sense of the cycles and rhythms, and that they reflect only a week, not a unit, a month, a term, or a year. I have found that working with student teachers to imagine a week works much better than writing an individual lesson plan, however. It alerts them to the issues of cycles and rhythms that Connelly (1985) argues will determine their professional success; it tends to make them better prepared in planning the curriculum around activities; it tends to make them more flexible and consequently more sensitive and more authentic in their interactions with students as they teach their planned lessons. From 30 years ago, I still feel the frustration of having turned in a lengthy lesson plan to my supervising teacher only to be told it was still not sufficiently detailed while I realized that it had detracted from the time I needed to plan for the other courses I was teaching that year. I honestly do not know of anyone who spends more time than I do thinking through how I am going to deliver a lesson, but I continue to find that the most important considerations are not the logic of the sequence of content so much as the pacing of the instruction so that I can maintain students' interest and adapt to their needs. The research suggests that I am not atypical; I conclude that we need to prepare student teachers to excel in the kind of planning experienced teachers have found works best.

Notes on Pacing

You will have a maximum of 180 days in a school year to teach your curriculum. During this time, you will sequence instruction in some logical fashion, building from the simple and basic to the more complex, and you will continually expand the scope of your curriculum coverage. The expanding spiral offers an apt metaphor for how your curriculum will build on itself both outward and upward. This is true whether you move from first position to an actual performance in ballet, from a simple somersault to a gymnastics routine, from a simple sentence to a term paper, from musical notation to performance, from Adam and Eve to contemporary issues. Often, the textbook you use will provide much of this spiral of scope and sequence.

On a week-to-week basis, however, I believe the psychology of your classroom needs to dictate your choice of lessons. This involves keeping your class both interested and serious. To do this, you need to balance constantly the type of activities you use. Ordinarily, you should not follow a test period with a lecture, a fun activity with a film, a small group activity with a competition, a lecture with a guest speaker, a game with role-playing. You need to balance individual, small group, and full class activities. You need to balance lectures, tests, discussions, and activities. When your lesson has been "outrageous," you need to come back with something sober. When your lesson has been most rigorous, you need to come back with a change of pace. And you should move from an activity before it has become too boring and while students would still like to be doing it.

I like to consider the following:

- At least once a week, do something with media. After students leave school, the media (not texts) will be their primary source of information. From newspapers, tapes, radios, TV, film, the telephone, journals, magazines, videotapes, even film strips, there must be something that relates to your subject matter in a meaningful way.
- Virtually every week, include the variety of individual, small group, and large group work. Variety is the spice of life.
- Every week, have something genuinely fun; something highly esoteric; and some normal stuff in between so that there truly is something for everyone.
- Every week, kids should read, write, speak, and listen, regardless of what your subject matter is. It's the writing and speaking that tend to be neglected. The writing takes time to grade, and you give up some classroom control when the students speak. Pay the price; it's worth it.
- You cannot ignore traditional standards of academic excellence. Include them. But don't hesitate to bring some divergent activities and their divergent standards of success into the classroom so that every student has an opportunity to be successful and everyone finds something that he or she isn't best at in the class.
- You don't have to have a quiz or test every week. Have some assignments that are done just for themselves.

Although I have heretofore emphasized the planning of the class period and the school week, I conclude this section on pacing the curriculum with a description of the prototype Larry Giacomino and I derived to characterize the day, the week, the term, and the year, and what we found to be effective pacing practices of good teachers. Although there is some repetition here, there is a logic to how I've presented organizing and pacing the curriculum. As a beginner, you will probably want to start with the ABCs. Once you are successful with the class period, you will want to start organizing and planning for the rhythms of the week. Once you become comfortable with the week, you will want to become sensitive to the large picture, the cycles and rhythms of a school year. If you are having problems, fall back to the more basic unit of teaching, whether it is the week or the day.

What if you ignore these observations? As Larry says, "Some teachers never figure it out . . . for example they continue to give Friday tests in afternoon classes during football season, then are frustrated on Monday when 14 football players and cheerleaders have to make up tests."

Or, as my friend, high school English teacher Mike McDermit, asks, "How do you feel about gravity?" Figuring out these pacing issues influenced, if not dictated, by the school's rhythms are critical for avoiding burn-out and thriving in teaching!

Parameters of School That Influence Pacing

The day.

- What students have done before they come to class has a tremendous effect on a class period. (Thus, an effective teacher must be prepared not merely to set a tone for the class but to change one.)
- Teaching is like flying an airplane. The greatest danger is in the take-off and landing. (Thus, an effective teacher must have methods of assuring an effective beginning and ending to a class period.)

The week. There are fairly typical patterns to a full week of school.

- Monday is usually the day students are the most sedate (a relative term). They have, for the most part, slept in later on Saturday and Sunday, so at least for the Monday morning classes, students may not be fully awake. This is often the day that is the best for the more teacher-centered, formal presentation of subject matter.

- Tuesday is often the day students are most likely to make a serious contribution. Students work independently or in groups better on this day than any other. Effective teachers often plan their most involving academic activity on this day.
- Wednesday. Hump day. This is a good time for seat work. Students tend to do what they are told but are not likely to have a lot of patience for teacher talk or working with each other.
- Thursday. Students are still able to focus their attention on the subject at hand. This is often a good day for testing.
- Friday. This is usually the most chaotic day of the week. School activities are most often scheduled on this day and absenteeism is the worst. This is a day the effective teacher uses the most intrinsically rewarding lesson, the lesson with the most pizzazz, the most stimulating, involving, innovative, interactive.

The term and year. The term and year have inevitable cycles. The year starts with the highest optimism and enthusiasm in September, but these gradually wane until a dramatic drop near December and the winter break. Some of the enthusiasm is renewed and regained in January, it wanes by spring break, and it vanishes by June 1.

Problematic days. Other times that signal probable problems include all Fridays; days before a vacation, especially Thanksgiving, winter break, and spring break; the day before, during, and after report cards; all days after June 1; hump days; days when students hit some temporary wall (that often looks like it will be permanent); days with assemblies; days after tests; minimum days; days of major school events such as dances and football games.

Optimal days. These are days without such "problems." The day before exams is particularly promising. Optimal days also tend to be relatively early in the week, the semester, the year.

Pacing Practices of Good Teachers

- Effective teachers tend to concentrate their most important, most difficult, most rigorous material into the optimal days of teaching.
- Effective teachers tend to use the more enriching classroom activities on the more problematic days. They especially avoid testing on problematic days.

- Effective teachers open their classes with an activity that helps students settle into the day's class and have something inherently interesting to keep their attention if the lesson happens to end early.
- Effective teachers have an intuition about what types of activity their students are prepared to do.
- Effective teachers believe variety is the spice of life and vary material—the most difficult and least difficult material, the esoteric and commonplace, the rigorous and fun, the teacher versus student-centered activities; listening, speaking, writing, reading; the individual, small group, full class; the most essential with the enriching; the various media.

Lesson Plans

Teachers, in fact, do not write formal lesson plans. This does not mean that they do not spend inordinate time planning. If you are required to write a lesson plan, however, you might find the almost instant lesson plan formats in the Resources section quick, convenient, yet meaningful.

I include these sample formats in case you run into a situation where someone requires you to write a lesson plan. These can be very helpful in writing meaningful lesson plans in a minimal amount of time. I know of no teacher who actually writes lesson plans, and I don't know of any good reason to master a technique that you don't plan to use. But if you are in a bind and have to have one, you might as well know how they look. As Zahorik (in Wittrock, 1985) points out, teachers plan lessons in different ways. More often than not, I start with what I want my students to do and then think about why. I think of myself as a very organized teacher. I spend a lot of time thinking through how I think a lesson might develop. But writing down the name or title of each activity for each class and the assignments is about all I have time for.

Earlier I discussed the benefits of A, B, and C activities. If you don't plan, you are likely to fail. But spending inordinate time writing lesson plans does not seem the best way to spend your planning time. Beginning teachers who write out lesson plans are probably the ones who don't need to do so, and those who don't are the ones who do need to do so. Just remember the adage that failing to prepare is preparing to fail.

Looking back at my own written plans from my first years of teaching, I cannot tell exactly what it is that I taught. But I can tell that I typically had an A, a B, and a C activity with a key word in my plan book that reminded me of what I had to do that classroom period. Again, failing to prepare is preparing to fail.

Grading, Evaluation, and Assessment

I have often thought the reason I continued my study of education was because of the injustices I felt because of thoughtless grading practices of my own teachers. Students take grades seriously, and this is an area that needs far greater teacher attention. This section is designed to make you more savvy about the implications of different approaches to grading.

Grading can be a very helpful way of motivating students, helping them to improve performance and evaluating your own progress in teaching. It can also be a nightmare. What I would like to emphasize in this section is that more than any other factor, grading reveals your own personal sense of justice and worldview. Some of the worst nightmares that I have heard were what teachers did to students with grades. Out of 1,000 possible points in a course (and you can be assured that with that many possible points in a course, not every test question is statistically reliable or educationally valid), I know of a student who did not graduate because of a 1 point difference between a D- and a F. Give me a break! The teacher even bragged about this grade in the faculty lounge as an example of maintaining standards. Ycch! I know you have to draw lines somewhere, but evaluation is such an inexact science, you must give students the benefit of some doubt.

Does your worldview allow time to learn? I know of a student who started off poorly in a course but had all As during the second half, including on the cumulative final. She got the hang of it midway. The teacher gave her a B. Give me a break!

I do not want anyone reading my book who would act like these two teachers. Their worldviews, to my mind, are sadly restrictive and suggest that they had experienced that there are never any breaks or allowances in life, that any error or omission causes irreparable damage. But even if that has been their experience, shouldn't they at least try to change it for others?

My point to you, as Jim Herndon (1971) says, it is you who puts the grade on the report card. You can use a point system, but don't hide behind it. Use some judgment. My daughter earned a B because a substitute teacher in her math class explained things incorrectly and the poor grades she received those 2 weeks counted as much as her A work during all the weeks her regular teacher was there. That stinks. Surely you can use better discretion than that.

I have an example that can prove how important it is to think through what your grading policy should consider. For simplicity's sake, pretend you have to give a student a grade based on only two grades, and that the two grades are at least potentially equally important. On the first grade, the student, for whatever reason, turns in a blank paper for a grade of 0. On the second grade, the student earns 100% and also earns 4 of 5 extra credit points. What grade should the student receive? According to how you average the grades, the grade could be an A, B, C, D, or F.

How can that be? Let me show you five of the ways these two grades could be computed. First, you could add the points and divide by 2. 104 plus 0 equals 104, divided by 2 equals 52, which under most systems equals an F.

Second, you could convert the points to letter grades on an 11-point scale, with an F getting no points, a D- 1 point, through to 11 points for an A. The 104 converts to an 11, the F to a 0, but the average of that total is 5.5, which is a C or C+, according to whether you round up.

Third, you could use a 12-point scale, with the 104 being equal to an A+ and a 12, meaning the average is a 6.0 and a C+.

Fourth (and if you do keep points, I highly recommend you do this because the only alternative is that one very bad test becomes a millstone on a cumulative point total), you could always give students the benefit of the doubt and award any F with the grade of the highest number of points an F would have earned, usually a 59. A 104 plus 59 divided by 2 equals 81.5, and a grade of B- or even B.

Fifth, if the tests are cumulative and there may have been a good personal reason the student turned in a blank paper on the first exam, you could let students drop one exam. In this case, the student would receive the grade of A. And if you were only a little forgiving, you could decide against failing the student and give the student at least a D.

So, what grade should you give this student? I don't believe in theoretical grades. I would want to know the student, the situation, the class, the context. And I'd want to use the system that fits my educational philosophy. I would want my system to reflect my values. Because I do give cumulative finals, I would not likely give this student lower than a B- in any circumstances. I certainly believe the student deserves at least that much reasonable doubt.

I generally look at all student records from a variety of methods and give the students the benefit of the method that gives them the highest grade. Especially when I find that I have written a particularly difficult test, I curve the grades. Another problem with using simple point scores is that on one test an A might be 94 points, but on a very difficult test, an excellent score might be 78. Unless you convert those points to grades and then use something like the 11-point scale described above, the student with these two top grades will not be recognized as having earned the highest scores in a semester's worth of running point scores.

There have been a few times where I have felt that a student received a slightly higher grade than I may have felt he or she truly earned. But in the long haul, I feel better about having erred on the side of generosity than stinginess. I resist grading by sentiment, but I am equally concerned about grades that are arbitrary, without regard for the machinations of the system we've chosen and that don't do what we personally want our system to do.

Grades and Worldviews:
An Exercise in Grading

As I said earlier, I sometimes think the primary motivation for my career in education is the injustices I felt as a student about my teachers' arbitrary and capricious grading methods. Once they had written a grade or number down, somehow it seemed to take on a separate life of its own. Although it is not easy for me to use numbers to explain concepts, I offer the following elaboration of the point I am making.

In Figure 2.4, I have created a fictional grade book record with 10 students and their (condensed) grade lines. I indicate the assignments and their points and six different methods of determining what these points might mean in terms of grades. I added the points and sorted them into six different ways of considering those points. In five of the examples, I offer systems that are sometimes used by teachers. I added a sixth that is not entirely without regard to points, but is based on my own personal judgment. Will anyone likely agree with me about each student's grade? No. Does one of the methods have more virtue than the others? Probably not. But I have found with my own student teachers that questioning each call helps each to realize how much judgment is involved in grading, how much variety there can be, and how strongly the final outcomes are determined by the teacher's worldview, not just some sort of objectification of numbers.

So, which method is the most fair? I am not a moral relativist. I tend to believe that with knowledge comes virtue. My hope in presenting this exercise to the larger audience is that it will have the effect of making some readers a bit more savvy, even a bit more modest, about their own practices. I know I have always lost a lot of sleep around grade card time. Thinking about all this does not make the job easier. But I am committed to the idea that the system has to work for my educational goals, not for me to conform to the system I have chosen, and that I am responsible for the grade I assign as the best possible measure of my professional judgment.

I offer the following as a prototype for you to adapt for your own grading philosophy and approach to writing exams.

A (Sample) Grading Policy

Philosophy

Grades have the potential of both motivating students and giving important information about their quality of work. A grade of C indicates that a student has met the basic objectives of the course; a grade of B indicates consistent, accurate, and quality work; a grade of A indicates particular distinction. Grades of D and F indicate a range of possible problems that will be followed up individually.

Grading

Records of assignments, homework, test scores, and the like will be kept. Sometimes percentages such as 90% and above reflect a grade in a traditional manner, but on more rigorous exams, standard scores or a curve may be employed. By professional discretion, a student may have a test dropped; a grade converted from a point system to a letter system; an important test weighted more heavily. If this is done for one student, it will be done for all students, with students receiving the higher grade if multiple systems result in discrepancies (e.g., if grading on a curve results in a higher grade than grading by the point system).

STU	E1	IC	HW	IC	HW	E2	IC	HW	IC	IC	HW	IC	FE	1 %	2 %T	3 ATP	4 D1T	5 TFE	6 Individual Judgment	Range of Grades*
1	26	7	7	7	7	81	7	7	7	7	7	7	81	64.5	74.3	67.0	77.3	70.0	Drop a test/more weight to exams B−	D+, D, C−, C, C+, B−
2	75	8	8	8	8	75	8	8	8	8	8	8	75	76.2	87.9	78.7	76.7	75.8	I value consistency B−	C, C+, B−, B+
3	65	0	3	7	6	77	7	6	8	9	9	8	95	75.0	86.5	77.5	78.3	81.7	I value getting there A	C, C+, B−, B, A
4	12	8	8	7	9	81	8	6	10	9	8	8	82	64.0	73.8	66.5	81.3	70.0	Forgive a test, especially the first test B	D, C−, B−, B
5	60	6	6	6	6	60	6	6	6	6	4	6	60	59.5	68.6	62.0	59.3	59.7	Probably hard-working kid going nowhere in school C−/C	F, D, D+, C−
6	0	3	0	5	6	55	0	6	7	7	0	6	65	45.0	51.9	47.5	60.0	51.7	I rarely give Ds but this is a good bet	F, D−, D
7	75	9	9	8	10	90	8	10	10	9	9	9	91	86.7	100.0	89.2	90.7	88.2	Improvement and performance A−	B+, A−, A
8	70	10	10	10	10	71	9	8	10	9	8	9	68	75.5	87.0	78.0	78.0	73.0	Works hard, not a good test-taker; hardest call C+	C, C+, B+
9	50	10	0	9	3	75	7	2	10	8	10	10	100	73.5	84.7	76.0	81.3	82.3	You eventually got this person's attention. With a bear of a final, this is an A	C, B, A
10	80	8	9	8	8	79	9	7	8	7	8	9	78	79.5	91.6	82.0	80.0	79.0	Evaluation is inexact, have to round up B−	C+, B−

Figure 2.4. Hypothetical Grade Book: Six Approaches to Grading

*Assuming the traditional grading scale

E1 = Exam 1
E2 = Exam 2
HW = Homework
FE = Final exam
IC = In-class assignment
% = Percentage of 400 point total
%T = Percentage of top score (347)
ATP = Add 10 points to original point total
D1T = Drop 1 test (300 total points)
TFE = Triple final exam in weight

90-100 = A
80-89 = B
70-79 = C
60-69 = D
0-59 = F

Basics on Writing Tests and Exams

First, have some humility about your exam. Professional test writers are only expected to write four to eight good test items a day. You are not likely to spend 5-10 days writing a 40-question exam. Consequently, (1) reserve ahead of time the right to drop questions that prove to be poor ones (regardless of whether a few students happened to answer them correctly), and (2) don't let a final grade be determined by a point or fraction of a point.

Second, tests and points are meant to help you be fair. But never forget that you chose the questions, you are the true measuring stick, you are the one who puts the grade on the paper. Students will prefer your acknowledgment of that responsibility to getting a grade on an arbitrary point total.

Third, there is an art to writing exams. Common errors in writing exams include a tendency only to test for memorization; a tendency to write items that are easy to write instead of testing the balance of material covered; a tendency to test for the arcane instead of the most important material. I personally believe that about 60% of tests should "measure" the most basic objectives that virtually all your students should get completely right. This 60% reminds all students of how much the entire class has learned. The remaining 40% should be based on such characteristics as rigor and robustness. Think of this 40% as giving students feedback about their readiness for the University of California (or Pepperdine).

Finally, some students will finish your test much more quickly than others. Essay questions will make this even more likely. Plan ahead for what you expect next of those who finish early.

P. S. You might be able to use the same test for consecutive periods, but only if you do not allow any student to leave the room before the next class arrives. Other than that, be assured that much of your test will have been described in detail to subsequent class members.

P. P. S. Count out loud the number of tests you give out and collect to help you with test security.

P. P. P. S. If questions are not weighted the same, you must let your students know that at the start of the test.

The Distinction Between Formative and Summative Evaluation

One of the most basic distinctions in the area of evaluation is between formative evaluation and summative evaluation. The idea of formative evaluation is that there is still time to make changes in your course. The summative evaluation is the final determination at the end of the course. Often, the summative evaluation is thought of as the final exam, but it also includes the teacher's final judgment about the quality of the student's work for the entire course; in a sense, summative evaluation also includes the student's final judgment about how successful the teacher has been.

I argue elsewhere the advantages of a cumulative final exam. By allowing any student who can pass the final exam to at least pass your course, you ensure that students will attend at least to your most basic course objectives and that you can still be on their side up until the last minute, regardless what point system may be benefiting other students who are more conscientious along the way. As you can tell from my section on grading, I do not think there should be but one way to earn a final summative evaluation. My analogy is to baseball's hall of fame. Some athletes make the hall of fame based on as few as 10 brilliant years, whereas others make the hall of fame for general excellence over a much longer period of time. Students who do great work on the most important assignments and students who do excellent work throughout the term can both get summative evaluations from me that include the grade of A.

Student Evaluations of the Teacher

Whether your school has a student evaluation process or not, you can be well served by asking students to evaluate your own work. I recommend that sometime just before you give your evaluation to students to fill out, you do a review of your course for them, not only of the topics but how you have organized the course and how you intended certain activities to work. If your school does not have an evaluation form, you might consider asking at least the following questions:

On a 5-point scale, 5 being high and 1 being low, please evaluate how descriptive the following statements are:

Part I: The Teacher
1. Shows interest and enthusiasm for the course. Comments:
2. Is prepared for class and makes good use of class time. Comments:
3. Presents course material in a clear and engaging manner. Comments:
4. Is an excellent teacher. Comments:

Part II: The Course
5. Is well organized. Comments:
6. Textbook and other readings assignments are appropriate in content and difficulty. Comments:
7. Tests and other evaluations are appropriate in content and difficulty. Comments:
8. Assignments are reasonable and appropriate in content and difficulty. Comments:
9. Is demanding in comparison to other courses. Comments:
10. Has increased my knowledge and understanding of the subject. Comments:
11. Is excellent. Comments:

Part III: The Overall Class Experience
12. Has enhanced my ability to think clearly, logically, independently, and critically. Comments:

The student comments are often more helpful than a numerical score. The entire process of teacher evaluation is more a measure of quality of life in the classroom than it is of actual learning. Statistically, the best question is question 4, about your excellence as a teacher. All the other questions will tend to correlate with that answer. If you add up all your scores to find an average, you should not overinterpret this score. These are small sample sizes, and one or two scores can skew your results up and down. Classes have different personalities. A 4.6 from one class might have been harder earned than a 4.8 from another. If the entire school doesn't do such an evaluation, you won't have a comparison group. If you do not have a comparison group, if you have an average score of less than 4.0, you probably need to work on getting along with your class better because that is the primary factor in your scores. A 4.4 means you are doing quite well. To move into the category with the teachers the students regard as superstars, you'd probably need to be above 4.7.

Teachers who do not get good scores tend to argue against the validity of these evaluations. My argument is that because you are there for the students, their evaluations are to be taken seriously. I also know that you cannot possibly get the highest scores without protecting your "weak" students but also challenging your best academic students. Despite allegations otherwise, you cannot get top-drawer scores by being an easy grader. For the top scores, all your students have to have found you fair, but your top students must also find you demanding and rigorous to give you their highest ratings.

Student evaluations are often given at the end of a semester or year. There's no reason, especially for a beginning teacher, not to give them out early as a formative evaluation. The scores and comments may very well give you the feedback necessary to make some midcourse adjustments and give students the clear signal that you are serious about your teaching and your concern for their overall well-being.

A Discussion of Assessment With Sample Assessment Techniques

My biggest concern about the enthusiasm for assessment, especially formative assessment, is how time-consuming it tends to be. I have before me a 427-page book on assessment. The length alone can be daunting. My message continues to be that, until you have established consistency and a basic competency in your classroom, you should spend most of your time finding worthwhile activities your students can manage and will mostly appreciate, and double-checking that your procedures and expectations for classroom behavior are appropriate.

This particular book that I am looking at has dozens of potential assessment techniques that you might use. In fact, I have used many of them myself. By now I am probably at a point in my career where I could get most of them to work. Empty outlines, minute papers, pro and con grids, one-sentence summaries. Each device can work toward assessment. As a student, however, I would want to know, "Are we going to be graded on this?" For these informal assessments, the answer must be no. So you have a problem. Some of the students probably won't want to do these assessments. Is this a problem? Is it a discipline problem? If so, it is one you created.

You certainly want regular feedback. Assessment is a good idea. But avoid making students do what may be seen as busy work. I have to admit that personally I am not very interested in trying the dozens of devices that have been developed as assessment techniques. If I do use a technique, I want it to be as organic as possible, a device that fits into what I do naturally. Recognizing that there are dozens of informal assessment techniques, I will describe seven approaches I have taken.

1. When I taught continuation school, Art Walsh and I developed *AAP*. It stood for analyze, assess, plan. Any time we had a problem that seemed to affect everyone, we called an AAP meeting. Everyone had agreed that when even a small minority of us, students or teachers,

thought we had a problem, everyone consented to coming to the AAP meeting. Perhaps some group felt we needed to be nicer to each other than we had been recently. We would meet, analyze what was going on, assess whether we thought changes were needed, and, if we thought changes were needed, plan something everyone would agree to do. I've always been for assessment, but only when there is a perceived need for such an assessment, not just because we have discovered a lot of new ways of doing it.

2. Once a semester, I use a technique sometimes referred to as *cognitive map making*. For a final review before my final cumulative exam, I ask students to draw a cognitive map that attempts to place all our important subject matter considerations into some sort of visual relationship with each other. From experience, I know that everyone benefits somewhat from trying to make their individual map. Further, I know that some will do a much better job of drawing a conceptual map than others. This is an assignment that takes advantage of small groups. I have groups of five talk about their individual maps, which causes them to undertake this as another review of our course material, and to choose the one map they think might help the rest of the class most. After the small groups have picked their best map, they share the best with the entire class. We try to decide which of these maps might be most helpful to the most students. If we have one that is especially helpful, I make a photocopy for each of the students to use as a review tool before the final exam. This is definitely an assessment technique. It also makes a good class activity.

3. At least once a quarter, I ask students to write down 10 questions about some aspect of the course. I promise them that they will not have to answer these questions on any kind of exam. They do not have to know the answer to the question. I want questions that show their best thinking. I have consistently found these questions the best indication of what kind of thinking the students are doing about the course. Whereas tests tend to turn up what students fail to learn, these questions are a great indication of what they are learning and reflect the great range of outcomes that occurs from the same course and teacher.

4. Although I find most checklists too arbitrary in what is included and excluded, I do not hesitate to give students the basic outline of the particular subject from the College Board's (1983) outline; then I ask students which areas they feel need greater attention. That is an important and inclusive list, so it works well for assessment.

5. Once in a while, I don't mind giving students a list of tasks. This isn't exactly an assessment because it is only an indication of

whether the students say they did the task. But I often want students to complete a range of activities that I do not want to grade. I consider it a part of their funding of experience. For example, because I want to make my curriculum as "real" as possible, I might want students to talk to someone, watch a documentary, see a movie, read a magazine article, look for something in a newspaper, find something in the library, draw something, interview someone, and so on. Perhaps all this needs to be done within a time period. I have neither the time nor the energy to evaluate how well they do these assignments, and besides, the assignments are supposed to be as intrinsically interesting as possible, and I have worked very hard to see that students see these activities as part of their funding of experience. A checklist keeps students reminded of what they need to do. After they have done it all, I may have an open-ended question (Eisner, 1991, refers to this as *expressive outcomes*) that asks them to write down what they learned from this experience. They can solidify a grade with this kind of assignment. The grade of A will still be reserved for the more conspicuously academic assignments. And although a task checklist isn't necessarily an assessment per se, the willingness of students to do this is an indication of how well you have made all this meaningful.

6. There is no better assessment technique than simply stopping and asking your class for its opinion. If you are teaching *Lord of the Flies,* and it has worked with every other class but it isn't working with this class, stop and ask students about their experience. Make sure a wide variety of students talk. Give them time to be thoughtful in their answers. Listen to what they say. You might need to wrap up this book early and go on to something else. You need not be defensive, just open.

7. Finally, I am humbled by the good advice individual students can give. You need to develop some savviness about which students you can ask which questions, and you need to be sure you aren't asking them inappropriate questions that compromise them in any way. Individual students answering individual questions is in my mind the best source of assessment information. If you know that two students are good friends, you can say to one of them, "I don't want you to divulge any confidences, but is there something I need to do to get Tim back on track?" If you see that one student is floundering, you can say "What do I need to do to help you be successful?" If you need to make a decision about what to teach next, you can ask a student, "What's worked best for you this year, I'd like to try to repeat something like it?" Your own students are your best resource once you learn to ask them good questions. Finding moments to talk with students one on one or in small groups can be exceedingly helpful in countless ways.

There are other techniques I have used in assessment. I still go back to my first couple years of teaching. Assessment was daily but mostly informal, because what I learned that day was likely to change what I'd do tomorrow.

Formal Evaluation:
The Messages Grades Send

Next to poorly handled discipline situations, the quickest way to get into serious trouble as a teacher is with the grades you assign. Teachers who give more than an occasional F are usually failing to teach effectively or are writing exams that try to catch what students didn't learn instead of tests that measure what was learned. I rarely give the grade of D. Passing students, including me as a former student of French, see this grade as an insult. A C- sends a similar message without the insult. Students still have to get a higher grade somewhere else to graduate. In a sense, you can think of the C as recommending a student to the community college, a B to the state college, and an A to selective colleges and universities. The parents who want their children to qualify for the University of California or its equivalent are the most likely to complain to the principal if you give students a grade lower than an A. You should have a strong rationale for the difference between a B and an A. That's why I recommend a wide variety of assignments that can help everyone pass your class, but a very clear rationale about the standards for your most demanding tests and papers. Again, the basic outline from the College Board (1983) is a great place to start as you try to explain to a college-bound student the reason he or she earned a B instead of an A. In truth, it isn't very easy to explain the difference between a B and an A. Often there isn't anything wrong with a B so much as it lacks the academic "robustness" of an A.

Later in this chapter, I share some of the basic concepts regarding testing and grading that should help you with the methods you use for making the distinctions among your C, B, and A students. I follow that with a list of the most common errors that you should be careful to avoid in testing and grading. I do not think that students are more virtuous for going on to college, but their opportunities will improve if they do so. Although I am most concerned about the learning each of my students does, I cannot be oblivious to the fact that I am teaching at a school that will prepare or fail to prepare a student for further study. Although there is more subjectivity to grading than is commonly realized, there is more agreement about what constitutes a successful academic test or paper than there is about most other classroom assignments. I think it is unconscionable to write poor tests and then give a grade that negatively influences a student's future opportunities.

Grades have the potential of both motivating students and giving important information about the quality of their academic work. Recognizing that grades are often used in helping students gather information about their interests and aptitudes, and that these same grades are often used for determining students' future academic opportunities, this means that grades must be honest, accurate, and fair.

Two further considerations about philosophy of testing and grading are germane here. First, because the student is the heart of the educational process, and the encompassing goals of the school entail far more than mere academic aims, teachers are expected to respect students on the basis of personal character, independent of strictly academic achievement status. Second, teachers must be careful in balancing what each student has learned versus the competing need to differentiate among all the students in terms of their academic performance. (This is, in a sense, the difference between testing for what was learned versus testing for what went unlearned.)

A More Expansive Overview of the Issues Surrounding Grading, Assessment, and Evaluation

I begin my first class of the new semester in my college curriculum and methods course with the earlier exercise on grading. Although logically the issue of grading follows the issues of objectives, teaching strategies, and tests, I believe that the issue of grading has the greatest emotional import, so it is a great place to start a class about teaching. In a split second, I can recall the teacher who assigned 2 points in a 10-point essay to writing down that the issue in question occurred during the time period we were studying. I felt that adding that detail was superfluous. What about the thoroughness of my answer? Those 2 points were the difference between an A and a B. I'm still bitter.

Having written about grading and test writing, let me now give you my subjective overview of the issues about evaluation.

First, recognize that most of the debate about assessment and evaluation is between conservatives and liberals. Conservatives emphasize standardized tests. They want that kind of assurance that students are really learning something to justify their hard earned tax dollars. Liberals know that you cannot measure all that's learned. They don't like to see their kids' performances reduced to numbers, especially because those numbers tend to correlate with socioeconomic status and thus tend to reinforce existing social inequities. Liberals' hearts are probably in the right place, but the parents of those same kids the liberals are worried about would also like some evidence that their children really are learning something. So liberals argue for stuff like authentic assessment and recommend evaluation techniques such as portfolios. School administrators, recognizing the legitimate claims of both conservatives and liberals, try to find compromises such as performance-based assessments using devices such as rubrics and checklists.

I am convinced that James Herndon (1985) is right. It is mostly talk. Teachers will do this year pretty much what they did last year regardless. But that does not mean that you should ignore the underlying issues regarding evaluation. Begin with the truth that evaluation is an inexact science and that students deserve the benefit of any doubt when it comes to a grade.

Standardized testing is a fact of life that will probably influence your students' futures. You must give them some help taking standardized tests. Minimally, students should always ask if there is a penalty for wrong guesses, and if there is not, they should fill in all the answers by the end of the exam. They should also learn how to pace themselves through a timed exam, knowing how many questions they need to answer per minute. Further, they should work through the exam quickly, marking and going back to difficult questions if they have time at the end.

I think that you should also help them interpret their results. One of the greatest misconceptions is about grade level. Grade level is essentially the average or middle score for that grade. By definition, 50% of all the students who took this exam will be below that score. 100% of the students cannot be in the top 50% of that grade. Students need some understanding of this. This does not mean that the bottom half of a class should be in a lower grade.

Quizzes and tests are usually the staple of a teacher's grade book, but they are only one way to grade, one way to evaluate.

Performance-based assessment, qualitative assessment, and portfolios are good alternatives in evaluation. In fact, they are personally more meaningful to the teacher and student and should be used. James Herndon (1971) is right, however, in saying that schools are primarily about separating the sheep and the goats. It is the letter grade you give a student that will have the most influence on which college the student is admitted to. If every student receives a high grade, you will not help

Harvard decide which students to admit. Students are much more willing to accept differential grades on exams and papers than on portfolios.

Of the many alternatives within evaluation, portfolios sound the best to me. Yet, everyone that I know who has tried them has given them up. Portfolios require too much paperwork, follow-up, and time to work over the long run. The same can be said for most performance-based objectives. Keeping track just takes too much time.

If your school requires these measures, follow them. But streamline the procedures as much as possible. I am more conscientious than most about students truly mastering important academic material, but I readily admit that when I have had to write objectives, I have tried to write objectives that students could probably already meet so that there was no question about my being successful. Why would anyone leave themselves vulnerable on purpose? Even so, I've read that no teacher has ever lost a job for his or her students failing to meet such performance standards.

That does not mean that I am not influenced by the alternative evaluation concepts. I do like to keep and/or have students keep their best work. Show it off at back-to-school night, put it up in the classroom, celebrate it. And if someone wants to call it a portfolio, so be it.

I also want all my students earning at least a C in my courses. Thus, I write certain tests as *criterion-referenced* tests. If each student passes these tests, the basic course objectives have been met, regardless how much missed homework or absences have occurred. In my class, everyone who masters the most basic material can earn at least a C. Despite my lack of fondness for objectives, I write out basic objectives so that each and every student is clear and has the security of knowing what the basic goals entail.

It is the Bs and As I am more particular about. It's the Bs and As that determine who is ready to go to the community college, state university, elite private school. You have to have certain papers and tests that give your most academically oriented students a chance to excel. Frankly, tests and papers are still the best ways for making those kinds of academic distinctions.

You cannot shirk your responsibility to give students honest feedback about the quality of their academic work. Your tests and graded work will be helpful in keeping you more or less objective. This is important. You must not fail in this responsibility.

But it is not truly the most important evaluation going on. I was recently annoyed by a teacher who said a student we both had was only his sixth or seventh best student. I told him, yeah, but in 10 years she will be the best of that group. I am positive that I am correct in this judgment. The reason it matters is that that student might need that validation to make it so. I won't give this student a higher grade because of that assessment, but I will be sure to share that assessment as part of an informal evaluation and on any letter of recommendation.

Students deserve your best effort at teaching and grading and your more informal evaluation of their strengths and weaknesses. But I also consider it my duty to identify the qualitative kind of contributions a student can reasonably make to a class and to cultivate those abilities. One student brings energy; another problem solving; another looks out for other students; another asks good questions; another goes with the flow. Once you start noticing such talent, you may not be able to give it a grade, but you can recognize the student for such contributions and cultivate those skills. Although you should be hesitant to place a grade on such skills and attributes, you are well advised to let students know how important EQ (emotional quotient) is to lifelong success and happiness.

Relevant Concepts Regarding Testing and Grading That You Should Be Familiar With and Should Influence Your Own Practices

(This material is highly derived from and influenced by Gage & Berliner, 1979.)

1. The standard error of measurement: The score of a student on any test is composed of "error" as well as the "true" level of the attribute we are measuring . . . thus, an observed score . . . is made up of true score and error score. The estimated amount of the error in a person's score is what we want to know. After we estimate the error, we can estimate a confidence band around the observed score and be pretty sure that a person's true score is within that confidence band. The standard error of estimate . . . provides us with the information needed to develop a confidence band for observed scores. . . . All this discussion of unreliability and error of measurement is designed to keep you cautious.

This concept is particularly important when assigning grades on a fixed point basis.

2. Normal distribution curves: Historically, the idea of A, B, C, D, and F grades was based on the idea that populations were distrib-

uted under what would ordinarily be a bell curve. The grade of C was thought to be a grade that represented "average" work represented by the middle of a bell-shaped curve. The thought that there are normal distributions is highly theoretical. In my mind, the students who stay in school are not a random population. I think the bell curve is pernicious if it is used to justify low grades.

3. Table of specifications: Research shows that teachers tend to ask test questions that are more easily written. The idea of a table of specifications is to ensure that there is an apt match between the balance of what was measured with what was taught. Check to see that your tests do not have too many points allocated to slivers of what you taught.

4. Criterion- and norm-referenced tests: Criterion-referenced tests mean that students are expected to demonstrate a certain level of knowledge or skill. Ordinarily, these exams are evaluated on a pass-no pass basis. Students who go beyond these expectations are treated the same as students who only meet the criteria. Norm-referenced tests differentiate among the levels of student success, and students receive letter grades accordingly. Criterion-referenced tests (perhaps for points instead of a letter grade) are often a neglected area of evaluation. As I indicated earlier, I like criterion-referenced tests at least for guaranteeing everyone has the likelihood of earning at least a C.

5. Formative and summative evaluation: Assignments and tests given before the final exam can be formative evaluations used for diagnostic instead of strictly graded activities. On the basis of this information, course direction can be altered. Summative evaluation, as symbolized by a final exam, is the final evaluation of student performance in that class.

6. Difficulty and discrimination: Statistical analyses of test items often reveal that some questions should probably be thrown out. Items that are too easy or too hard do not help differentiate among students' success. Items that the students who did the worst on the exam were more likely to get right than the students who did well are suspect. Before you give the test, get students to agree that questions that turn out to be poor questions will not be counted.

Common Errors in Testing and Grading to Avoid

1. Countless research studies have shown that tests often only measure very low levels of knowledge. Benjamin Bloom (see Gage, 1979) describes six levels of cognition that can be measured: knowledge, comprehension, application, analysis, synthesis, and evaluation.

Very often, the knowledge level, based on memorization, dominates tests.

2. Test items are often those that are easily written rather than those that measure the range of material taught. You should match the points given on the test with the material most emphasized in the class.

3. Often, tests are speed, not power, tests. Make sure students have adequate time to finish the exam.

4. Poorly written questions often measure reading or problem-solving skills instead of the academic concept meant to be tested. Is it a true measure of learning if your 8th grade test requires a 12th grade reading level?

5. In short answer exams, students with wrong answers are often overrewarded compared to students who merely leave the same question blank. This is especially true if you curve your results. Is giving 3 points for an entirely wrong answer fair if you gave 0 for an unanswered question?

6. If you have written a particularly difficult exam, it might be fairer, especially if you are using percentages, to use the highest grade in the class as a standard instead of the ubiquitous 60, 70, 80, and 90. If your "best" student has the highest grade, and it is an 82, might not that be an A, and 80% of that grade be a B-?

7. Tests often measure what was previously taught (in other classes or schools) instead of what was taught in that class per se. That's certainly not fair.

8. Extra credit is not extra credit if it is figured into a point score before a curve is made.

9. A zero on an assignment can be an albatross, a stone, an anvil, to a grade. Some find that giving a student the highest F on a blown assignment is fairer in the overall picture.

10. Because it is impossible to make each test you write equally difficult, convert point scores to letter grades (e.g., a score of 92 that was given the grade of A to a system that then recognizes that the A is worth 11 points, A- worth 10 points, a B+ 9 points, etc.).

11. Bias can creep into an evaluation in many ways. One of the most common in reading through exams is unintentionally setting higher standards for early tests or later tests. A way to avoid this is by shuffling papers during reading so that the place an exam comes up for your review varies.

12. Tests often measure points that are not the most relevant concepts of the course.

13. Any format you use will benefit some students more than others. For example, if the exam requires students to recognize certain

passages from texts, the exam may measure the single talent of recognizing text rather than the myriad of skills involved in mastering the subject matter.

14. If you are writing multiple choice exams, Nate Gage (Gage & Berliner, 1979) recommends these 12 points:
   a. The stem should focus on and state a meaningful problem rather than merely lead into a collection of unrelated true-false statements.
   b. The distracters should be plausible so that students who do not possess the achievement being evaluated will tend to select them rather than the correct answer.
   c. Use as many distracters as can be logically created.
   d. Do not hesitate to change the number of distracters from item to item.
   e. Use direct quotations rather than incomplete statements in the stem when it seems appropriate to do so.
   f. When possible, avoid repeating words in the alternatives; put them in the stem.
   g. The length and precision of the choices should not vary systematically with their correctness.
   h. The correct response alternative should vary from item to item.
   i. All choices should be grammatically consistent with the stem and with one another.
   j. There should be one and only one choice that experts would consider best.
   k. It is probably best to avoid using "none of these" as an alternative.
   l. Do not make tests so long that they become speed rather than power tests.

Writing good multiple choice items is very time-consuming. Professional test makers often write 4-8 items in a workday. Certainly a teacher might write a bit faster than that, but how fast? Publisher-produced test banks are usually not written by the textbook writers (and the poorer quality of the test items often shows).

Final Words About Grading

Nate Gage (Gage & Berliner, 1979) says about grades,

Students deserve the benefit of the doubt, given our imprecise measurement instruments and the importance sometimes attached to grades. . . . Grading and reporting on student performance is serious business. Teachers need to work hard to create a fair, humane, and easy to understand evaluation system. (p. 767)

∼ Motivating Students

Human beings are more alike than not. What you don't do, we probably don't want to do. What you learn from, we probably learn from.

(Herndon, 1971, p. 129)

I always think about motivation. Not only must I have material important for students to learn, I must ensure that they want to learn. As I mentioned earlier, Ralph Tyler once told me (how is that for name dropping?) that if he added a question to the four he raised in his classic book, *Basic Principles of Curriculum and Instruction* (1950), it would be a question about motivation. My own rule of thumb about motivation is that if I wouldn't want to do it, my students are not likely to either. Your teaching strategies will be useless if your students don't do their work.

How Do You Motivate Students?

Good teachers develop an uncanny sense of what their students will or will not do. The best list of factors in motivation that I have found is from Gage and Berliner (1979). They identify 13 environmental factors in motivation that are very helpful. They also identify five aspects of teacher authority that can be used in various combinations to affect motivation. Even then, the teacher must know what will work with his or her own students.

Gage and Berliner's (1979) list of environmental concerns with regard to motivation is as follows:

1. Use verbal praise.
2. Use tests and grades judiciously.
3. Capitalize on the arousal value of suspense, discovery, curiosity, and exploration.
4. Occasionally do the unexpected.
5. Whet the appetite.
6. Use familiar material for examples.

Planning Lessons and Teaching Strategies 87

Figure 2.4. Understand the power relationships between teachers and students.

7. Use unique and unexpected contexts.
8. Require use of what has previously been learned.
9. Use simulations and games.
10. Minimize the attractiveness of competing motivational systems.
11. Minimize the unpleasant consequences.
12. Understand the social climate of the school.
13. Understand the power relationships between teachers and students.

In their description of power relationships, Gage and Berliner (1979) note five different sources of authority: reward, coercive, legitimate, referent, and expert. In these regards, I have at times bribed (reward), threatened (coercive), and imposed rules (legitimate). With regard to referent authority, I have found that if you command respect, students will respect and even like you. If you want to be liked, you are in trouble. Expert power works well with most students, but sometimes you will find a student knows more about something than you do. The key is realizing how much power the teacher has and to use these types of power effectively.

Although I find the Gage and Berliner (1979) lists exceedingly helpful as reminders, they are somewhat more descriptive than telling. A teacher could plan to use any of the factors and still fail miserably. These factors in motivation work only when they work for your own particular, unique class. Something that will surprise one class will fall flat in another class. Nothing works outside of knowing your own students.

Certainly the standby for motivation of students is "You will be graded on this" or "It will be on the test." These work for all the students some of the time, some of the students all the time, but never all the students all the time. These represent a big stick, but it must be used sparingly.

My next major suggestion evidences my own immaturity. I was only somewhat surprised in interviews I conducted with teachers with reputations as strong teachers that they shared my more juvenile tastes. By that I mean that they, too, move on in the lesson or unit when they themselves are getting a bit bored. I think that they have trained themselves to get bored even more quickly than their students. James Herndon recognizes that students will not want to do something that you do not want to do yourself. Why would we think otherwise? The more resourceful you are, the more materials with potential that you gather, the more able you are to pick and choose accurately what will work with your class, the more impatient you become with yourself and the more willing you can be to move on.

A third suggestion is that you must set up and sell all your lessons. And you have to be honest. I offer the following examples of truthful comments that you might make to set up and sell your lesson:

- "This is hard, probably not everyone will be able to do it well. It will probably help sort out the A students."
- "As quickly as everyone can do this drill correctly, we will move on."
- "I think that you will like this activity a lot. But if it doesn't work out, we will stop it before it is otherwise over."
- "This will be a 12-minute lecture. It will be on the test. You will probably want to take notes. I will not go over 12 minutes with it. Look at the clock, exactly what time does that mean I will definitely stop? We will stop by then."

- "If you can handle this small group activity, we will do more of this type of interactive lesson."
- "This is something that will likely help you in other classes."
- "This is something other people would expect you to know."
- "The reason I want you to do this is . . ."
- "This is required. We have no choice. We can do it quickly or drag it out."
- "I really like this. I think it is very worthwhile, but I still want to know what you think after it is over."
- "This will help you get a job."
- "Impress your parents or guardians with this."
- "Do this or I will break your fingers."

Fourth, make your classes as "real" as possible. Having a good text students can read on their own helps free up more classroom time for activities. Always choose the most "vital" choice. Choose a person over a film clip, a film clip over a CD, a CD over a newspaper clipping, a newspaper clipping over the text for classroom activities.

Fifth, involve the students. The teacher my daughter most admires asks his students before each curriculum unit what resources they have that pertains to the subject. He finds it amazing how many relatives, friends, videos, CDs, artifacts, and so on turn up that are far better than what he otherwise has at his disposal. Also, have the students be as active as possible. Let them lead the drill, read the passage, make the presentation, participate in the small group, answer the question, introduce the guest. Mention students by name, refer to their past contributions, use them as examples, recognize them! They will be happier, you will be happier.

Sixth, be interested in your students. It almost makes me sad how generous and forgiving students will be with teachers when they show genuine interest in both their subject matter and their students. Such interest in students is too uncommon. Having read thousands of teacher evaluations, the three main teacher characteristics I find that students want are that the teacher (1) is knowledgeable about the subject, (2) has enthusiasm for the class, and (3) cares about the students.

Seventh, variety is the spice of life. My daughter's favorite teacher now has enough tricks of the trade that he says he never does the same thing twice. And successful teachers tell me that they always try to leave

Figure 2.5. Once you sincerely have a student's best interests at heart....

an activity before it starts to lag. Leave the students wanting more; don't wear the topic out.

Eighth, once you sincerely have a student's best interests at heart, you can cajole, harass, prod, poke, and foment that student to give his or her best effort. This is not the same as coercion, where your only goal is to get students to do what you expect.

Ninth, laugh a lot. I read somewhere that the average American laughs only five times a day. I find that hard to believe. Students should laugh more than that each class period.

Tenth, be willing to experiment to find out what does work with individual students and classes. Some classes need to be yelled at, some need to be challenged, all have a life of their own. The same strategy will not work all the time. The key is forcing yourself to be open to the truth of what you find. Only then can you adapt.

There are three groups of problem students that you need to be savvy about, especially with regard to motivation. The neglected students need lots of nurturing. Many working-class students see strict discipline as caring. For spoiled students, unearned nurturing is like gasoline on a fire. You need to be discerning about which students require what.

A lot of new teachers with privileged backgrounds are ill prepared to handle these realities. Their hearts go out, rightly, to students who have been so discouraged they require lavish support, reinforcement, and nurturing. That same teacher behavior does not work across the board. Some students see such teacher behavior as a sign of weakness.

I was the kind of kid whom if you yelled at me, I presumed you didn't like me. All kids aren't that way. As Herbert L. Foster (1974) points out in *Ribbin' Jivin', and Playin' the Dozens* (and he is quoting W. B. Miller),

> Since "being controlled" is equated with "being cared for," attempts are frequently made to "test" the severity or strictness of superordinate authority to see if it remains firm. If intended or executed rebellion produces swift and firm sanctions, the individual is reassured, at the same time that he is complaining bitterly at the injustice of being caught and punished. (pp. 240-241)

The guilt squeeze tends to work better with middle-class kids, and specific sanctions and punishments tend to work better with working-class kids. But, as with all generalizations, this isn't much help in figuring out your 30-40 students per class. You cannot predict which kids respond to which kind of discipline except through trial and error. As a beginning teacher, I found it hard to be tough in the face of vociferous complaints from students until I realized that a lot of kids equate such toughness and fairness with caring.

Certainly, the better you motivate your students, the fewer serious discipline problems you are likely to have. It is essential to realize that different motivational devices work with different students. The dual task is to discover as many motivational devices as possible and then to consider which will work best with your particular students.

Miscellaneous Tips on Teaching

The following is a list of tips. They are the tips that I have had reason to pass on the most often to new teachers. Many are repeated elsewhere in these pages. In this form, they are quick reminders and have greater prospect of being immediately useful. They are most likely to connect when they are answering a particular need. The key is their timeliness. I think you will find that this is a good list to review periodically.

Tips on Teaching Techniques

- When you are leading a class discussion and a student asks a question softly, be sure to repeat the question so everyone hears it. Tend to move away from a student you are talking to (while maintaining good eye contact) so that the student speaks more loudly and thus can be heard by everyone. Also, when you've asked a question that is simultaneously answered by multiple students, you will inadvertently hear only the correct answer. All the students may not know which of the many answers they heard was correct, however. Repeat a correct student answer.
- When asking students to read out loud, I recommend calling names, so everyone gets a chance, but allowing the student to choose not to read. This puts everyone on notice they might be called; allows you to avoid giving the toughest passage to the worst reader; and allows students an escape route from embarrassing themselves in front of the class.
- Minimize extra directions or repeating directions to the entire class. Circulate to see that your directions were understood properly.
- Don't ask poor questions such as "How many have read . . ." They tend to inculcate dishonesty.
- Variety is the spice of curriculum as well as of life. Vary your teaching strategies.

Tips on Teaching Procedures and Policies

- Homework should be assigned every weeknight, Monday through Thursday (or every week so that it could be done every night). If some students can master your objectives without doing all the homework, however, who cares? And if your students who can't or don't do homework learn most of your objectives, why not make it possible for them to at least pass your class? It should not be necessary to have done it all to pass your class.
- Minimize late assignments. Make your deadlines in advance to give the students plenty of time to turn the assignment in early. Encourage early submission. What if a student is absent? Even

if the student is quarantined, the mail carrier picks up mail once a day and that mail is postmarked that same day. If a student cannot bring or send in an assignment, accept it in the mail, but only with a postmark that meets the deadline.
- All your assignments do not have to be for a letter grade. Some can be criterion-referenced. If they meet the basic criteria, the student receives full credit. Excellence is its own reward. This allays a lot of fears and nit-picking about differences in grades on tasks with unclear criteria for success.
- A few students in most classes will try to get a competitive edge by missing your test; getting an excuse from their parents; and asking friends about what was on the test. You, by law, have to allow them opportunity to make up work missed because of an excused absence. Always make the make-up test different; try to make it harder. If the original was a multiple choice test, try to make the new one an essay test to minimize your time in rewriting a second test. Reward those who take the test as planned.
- The really time-consuming part of homework is assigning grades or points. Grades and points are always contested and thus take up valuable teacher time and energy. I like to review homework and mark it with four different marks: a plus for a special effort; a check-plus for a decent job; a check for a marginal effort; and a minus if the student turned in a paper that he or she may as well have not done. The letters approximately correlate with A, B, C, and D, but I tell students that they don't (and they don't know that I don't average them in as grades per se). Thus, homework can potentially make a difference in grades. A string of pluses and check-pluses will tend to improve a grade and give the student the benefit of the doubt. A string of minuses will do the contrary. This system helps reward the conscientious student without overdoing it and gives a little more slack to the student with little support at home.

Tips on Being Savvy

- Teach to your strengths.
- The overwhelming advantage of a cumulative final is that you can hold out to your worst student the prospect of still passing, if only barely, your course. Any other decision on your part invites a discipline nightmare from the moment the student

realizes he or she cannot pass your class to the last minute of that class. I know of an experienced teacher ending up in a fistfight with a student who had been told since February he couldn't pass the class. This does not justify the fight, but it did not surprise me.

- Never apologize in class about the curriculum. Don't ever tell students your lesson might not be as good as planned, or that you forgot to bring the tape recorder, or that the copy should have been clearer, or that you forgot their papers, or whatever you want to apologize for. Students are critical enough already without adding fuel to the fire and giving them the unintended message that you are incompetent. Leave apologies for personal matters.
- If you can get the class involved in a self-directed activity, you can spend time with individuals or small groups who need special help.
- Step outside your subject to solve whatever problems are in your way. If your class members aren't listening to each other, do a communications lesson regardless of your subject matter. If your talented chorus doesn't look like winners, teach poise.
- Make your learning environment attractive. Display student work. Highlight your subject matter with displays and posters. Students are likely to retain this material they are looking at while otherwise not paying attention.

Tips on Approaching the Subject

- The cardinal sin of an educator is to be boring. Make your class interesting; make the quality of life in your class agreeable.
- A rule of thumb on organizing your curriculum is to take the number of chapters in your primary textbook; divide that number of chapters by the number of weeks in the semester or year or the length of time the course lasts (usually 18 for a semester and 36 for the year). Plan to cover about that many chapters per week. Then try to bring that material to life as best you can in as many ways as possible. Cover the material effectively but as efficiently as possible. Use the remainder of the time for enrichment of that curricular material.
- Teach to your test. Your test should measure your objectives, so you should be teaching the skills you measure.

- Just like I think you should teach to your test (because it measures what you want students to learn), I think you should teach to your course evaluations. If it is important to organize your subject matter, point out how your subject matter is organized. If you want students to enjoy music, point out the times they are enjoying music. Help students make the connections between the purposes and the results. Then ask students how well your particular class makes those connections.
- Now that your lesson is exceedingly well conceived and prepared, you've still got to sell it to your class. "This will be really fun," or "interesting," or "helpful in college," or "keep you from flunking." It is much easier to sell something you believe in, but you need to sell it regardless.
- Don't make everything competitive.
- You don't have to cover in class everything you expect students to learn. That's what texts and homework are for.
- Students who can pass your cumulative final should be able to pass your class with at least a D. It proves they learned something, and you can keep at them, and on their side, until the very end.
- Teach your students how to study, read, and write for your particular subject area. Don't assume the English teacher or anyone else can do that for you.
- Don't teach it if you wouldn't learn it.
- A meaningful, activity-based curriculum works. From John Dewey (1938) to Leslie Hart (1978), educators have verified that we learn by doing.
- A well-taught class mitigates against discipline problems.

Teaching the Hidden Curriculum

By far the favorite academic concept I discovered after having taught a few years was that of the *hidden curriculum*. The hidden curriculum, a term coined by Philip Jackson (1968), recognizes that "schools socialize children to a set of expectations that some argue are profoundly more powerful and longer lasting than what is intentionally taught or what the explicit curriculum of the school publicly provides"

(p. 75). All your decisions about teaching and discipline have implications for the expectations that you are implicitly teaching your own students. Although the emphasis in this book is getting through the basics of teaching your subject and managing your classroom, the following summaries of some of the most basic work in the area of hidden curriculum may help you stay conscious of the overriding implications of your own choices as a teacher.

My personal experience confirms the conclusions of Jackson (1968) that the hidden curriculum is profoundly powerful and long-lasting. Unfortunately, much of the work in this area by scholars, including Jean Anyon (1980), Michael Apple (1977), Basil Bernstein (1975), Samuel Bowles and Herbert Gintis (1976), Robert Dreeben (1968), Elliot Eisner (1979), Henry Giroux (1979), Jules Henry (1965), Philip Jackson (1968), Dan Lortie (1975), Norman Overly (1970), and others (Sarason, 1982), is not included in teacher preparation programs. This short section on the hidden curriculum is only introductory, but should point you toward significant work when you have more time to reflect on your early teaching experiences. This section will introduce you to some of the terminology that may help you think through the issues of how you are advertently or inadvertently socializing your own students.

I agree with Elliot Eisner (1979) "that teaching is an art guided by educational values, personal needs, and by a variety of beliefs or generalizations that the teacher holds to be true" (p. 153). Certainly, my values include that teaching can be made more enjoyable and good gamesmanship is a way of increasing that enjoyment; that in terms of needs, a teacher must have a basic level of success before any more professional growth can possibly take place. I have a strong belief that there are no true prescriptions for any other teacher except reacting to what others have done and finding one's own way.

Jules Henry (1965) argues that schools teach the essential cultural nightmare: envy of success, fear of failure. I am determined not to emphasize this nightmare any more than avoidable. I admit that I am much more likely to emphasize envy of success than fear of failure. Part of my reason for this is vanity. If I intend to be the best teacher my students have ever had, very few of them should fail. Learning theory has shown us that students do not do their best work under great stress. Fear of failure may be helpful to students as they go out into the business world, but I emphasize my role as an educator and de-emphasize the fear of failure regardless of how realistic such lessons may or may not be in the economy.

Philip Jackson (1968) writes about three lessons of the hidden curriculum: power, praise, and crowds. His research indicates that students learn to defer to the teacher's power; they work for the teacher's praise instead of personal gratification; and they get used to being treated as part of a crowd instead of strictly as individuals. Certainly, these lessons have some use in getting students ready for the real world. They will most likely have a boss to whom they will defer, their work will be judged by company guidelines, and they will spend much of their lives waiting in lines. I prefer to take the edge off of these inevitable lessons. Gradually over my time with any group of students, I try to help them take more individual responsibility instead of simply deferring to my own authority. Although I accept what is inevitably students' expectations that I can perform any role necessary in terms of my status as a professional teacher, I want to implement more democratic expectations. I consider it a weakness that I too often praise students' performances in terms of my own tastes. I make a special point to spend more time asking students for their own appraisal of their own work. The larger the class, the harder it is to treat students in any way other than a crowd, but I often go down my class roll when my room is empty and do a mental check on whether I have had some sort of personal contact with each and every student over the past few days. When I realize I have not made a connection, I make a special point to initiate a contact with that student at the next possible opportunity.

Elliot Eisner (1979) argues that schools often teach compliant behavior, competitiveness, and a questionable sense of what is important. Certainly, the larger the class, the more compliant behavior may make the class seem easier to teach. But in the long run, my experience has been that once you channel a rowdy class, its level of achievement will be much higher, and the class will have been much more fun for you and for them. I give some rather obvious cues that I do not value compliance as much as others. I let students pick their own seats (at least until there is a problem); I don't have a set format for turning in homework or papers; I value the student who disagrees with me. That I have used the metaphor of the game plan for this book is but one indication of how much I love competition. But I also make my own attitudes toward competition very public. For example, I do not in any way limit the number of As in a class, so someone doing well can be helpful to other students in terms of figuring out how to do the work successfully. I also go over in class the Greek idea of competition: It is meant to be fun and to improve personal performance, not to be used to make invidious comparisons. Finally, I constantly ask myself whether students really need to be doing what I have planned. If a student challenges the worthiness of an assignment, the student may be right, in which case I concur and look for something truly worthwhile.

Robert Dreeben (1968) contends that schools teach students certain standards of behavior he calls "norms." He argues that schools teach students to do their own work by themselves; to achieve according to the teacher's expectations; and to accept being treated more impersonally that they are accustomed to being treated at home. Student expectations to do work independently is one of the more difficult issues I have faced as a teacher. It seems to be one of our culture's chief values. Yet, there is more and more evidence that cooperation is necessary in the workplace. Any teacher who remembers being a student is always worried about group work, that if there is going to be a group grade, all members of the group have to work to ensure the assignment is done properly. There are methods for team learning that can work very well, but these need more space than I have in this section. I encourage you to find ways to take the edge off this norm of independence by finding meaningful cooperative assignments, but be very careful how you grade them. In terms of whose expectations should be realized, you must be the one who knows what is customarily expected of students who have taken your subject. You cannot shirk that responsibility. I like giving creative assignments in which I ask students for their own assessment of their work. For me, this is usually for points instead of a grade, points that can be used to shore up a grade but not necessarily be used toward an A in the class (a grade that is still used to give a more specific message about strictly academic performance). As I have said before, I try to make my class as personal as possible given the limitations of class size. It's a reason I try to know all the names of my students by the end of the first week, if not the first day.

Jean Anyon (1980) discovered differences among working, middle, affluent professional, and executive elite schools, even if a course title is the same. She found that students are taught different concepts of work. Work in working-class schools tends to be mechanized and rote; work in middle-class schools consists of following the rules and getting the right answers; work in affluent professional schools involves creative activity; work in executive elite schools emphasizes developing one's analytic, intellectual powers. In the way schools teach work, they prepare students for different social classes. I have had students who demanded worksheets to fill out. That is a very working-class expectation. I do not think there is any particular moral superiority of one class or another, but there is differential social and economic opportunity. I give students worksheets, but I also tell them about Anyon's research. I want my students to have as many opportunities as possible. A working-class student who wants to go to Harvard needs to realize that there are different expectations. The student of someone from the executive elite class who wants to be an auto mechanic needs to realize that the expectations are different.

Giroux (1979) has identified a number of lessons of the hidden curriculum. Students learn to accept:

1. Rigid timetables
2. Unnecessary delays and denials
3. Tracking and social sorting
4. Hierarchical relations of dominance and subordination
5. The correspondence between evaluation and the arbitrary exercise of teaching power
6. The fragmented, isolated, and competitive interpersonal dynamics of the educational experience

I recommend trying to eliminate those lessons. It is a hope more than an assumption that by becoming conscious of these tendencies in the implicit curriculum, the hidden curriculum, we can become as conscientious about these lessons as we are about the lessons of the overt curriculum.

Michael Apple (1977) describes schools as teaching students to be competitive, tolerate ambiguity and discomfort, to accept arbitrariness, to conform, to define their scheduled activity as work not play, and to think of conflict as negative. I hope that by recognizing such tendencies, we can better avoid them. In terms of Apple's list, the distinction between work and play is the one that grabs my attention. The very fall my daughter started kindergarten, the very week I was teaching the Apple article in my own college course, my daughter came home from school and announced that her playroom was now to be called her workroom. From then on, her coloring and painting were thought of as more important, thought of as work instead of play. I regret the truth that she recognized. This book is about restoring more play in our professional work. In regard to Apple's point about conflict, I have tried with increasing success to have my intellect tell my emotions to realize what is true, that conflict can be very positive when handled openly and truthfully. Jenny Gray (1968, 1969) says that problem students will teach you the most as a teacher. This truth is never easy.

Bowles and Gintis (1976) found that schools reward students for perseverance, dependability, and consistency but not creativity and independence. I make a distinction between attention span and concentration span. Attention span means how long someone stays interested in something he or she has already found interesting. Many students can play video games for hours. Concentration span means learning to work on something after it has lost its inherent interest. However successful you are at making your subject matter interesting to your students, you will not be able to depend solely on their attention span. It is appropriate to work specifically with students on the issue of concentration and perseverance. If there is a skill that needs to be learned to be successful in your class, by all means you must make that skill an intentional part of your curriculum.

Paulo Freire (1970) asserts that schools teach students to be passive. His antidote is dialogue. I have taught most academic subjects at one level or another. There has always been something about those subjects that shows up in popular films and/or music. I enjoy asking students about their favorite films and music. I do not do this to be popular. I do find the conversations interesting. I don't try to turn those conversations to my own classroom interests. But I am likely to take something I learned in those conversations to my classroom to illustrate some academic point that needs a good illustration. Meanwhile, the lesson is about dialogue, about a willingness to learn from each other.

Finally, Henry Giroux (1979) believes that schools teach individualism, competition, fatalism, cynicism, distrust, dislike of theory, and respect for authority. Well, on the one hand Emerson's (1967) "Self Reliance" is my all-time favorite essay, and I do think of myself as a competitor. On the other hand, one of my favorite poems is John Donne's "No Man is an Island," and my favorite bumper sticker is "Question Authority." In the middle is that I love the concept of praxis and the dialogical relationship of theory and practice.

Again, my hope in briefly sketching these points of view about the hidden curriculum is that by beginning to develop a vocabulary to describe the hidden curriculum, you may more conscientiously choose appropriate strategies for the lessons you teach from the hidden curriculum.

Thus, I offer a sketch of some of the more prominent approaches to the issue of hidden curriculum. This list is suggestive, definitely not prescriptive. My primary aim is to stimulate the kind of thinking necessary for you to acknowledge the existence and effects of the hidden curriculum and for you to take more deliberate steps to use it purposefully. I think it is dangerous to leave the effects of the hidden curriculum to unconscious habits, precedents, and hidden influences. All your decisions have implications for that profound, powerful, and long-lasting curriculum that socializes our students. I accept Socrates's dictum that the unexamined life is not worth living. My intent here is for you to examine the lessons of the hidden curriculum, borrowing Paulo Freire's (1970) belief that we can develop our critical consciousness, love each other, and become more fully human. Although my emphasis in this book is in offering ideas that can be immediately helpful in teaching and managing your classroom, realizing the significance of your many choices is part of the joy of a career as a teacher.

Notes

1. Reprinted with permission from *Academic Preparaton for College.* © 1983, the College Entrance Examination Board. All rights reserved.

2. Reprinted with permission from Gose, M. D. (1989). "Making Small Groups Work." *California English, 25* (5).

3

Managing Classroom Behavior

You don't especially want students to obey you with fear because then they won't tell you important things like "The superintendent is coming down the hall to visit your room." It's better if they obey you in much the same spirit they would obey the captain of a team—because you're a good Joe and you're much better than they are at whatever you're doing.

(Gray, 1969, pp. 11-12)

This chapter is eclectic, addressing discipline from a number of tactical approaches. The level of specificity of each section is so different that the sections defy any obvious integration. Logically, the comments on philosophy of discipline should come first, but my experience is that your educational philosophy will evolve based on the tactics that actually work for you.

Thus, this chapter begins with expectations and procedures. Whether your expectations and procedures are written or tacit, explicit or implicit, you will have to identify them for each area. The list of areas for expectations and procedures is followed by my comments on the advantages and disadvantages of the ploys and strategies that I have used in setting my own informal policies. The assumption is that thinking through the issues about classroom management will help you make better choices.

The section on expectations and procedures is followed by Mike Myers' six rules. The reason for this order is strictly a matter of flow.

The expectations and procedures section is so straightforward, the humor of Myers' list seems appropriate as a change of pace. Hoping to have brought the issue of play back into the discussion, I follow Myers's list with physical ploys to affect student behavior. Just compiling that list was great fun. I sat down and tried to remember every physical mannerism that I had ever seen used to influence class behavior. The items are akin to the football linesmen who eat garlic before a game so that their breath is disgusting to try to get an advantage. It's a list of mostly physical behaviors that can affect a sudden change in student behavior. The difference between the football player and the teacher is that teaching is about successful play, but it is not about winning at the student's expense. In the classroom, you must play your leadership role well. In terms of gamesmanship, this is more like the quarterback growling at the halfback who missed a block than it is about taking advantage of the other team.

Having spent so much time emphasizing what you can do, it seemed time to follow those tricks of the trade with what not to do—20 classic teaching mistakes. How can you avoid these mistakes? You probably can't. But becoming aware of them may help you cut down on their frequency; minimizing unnecessary mistakes is another way of improving your classroom management.

I consider "Classroom Games and How to Play Them" my best insight into classroom interactions of my 30 years of teaching and observing classes. This is the section that gets to the heart of understanding the give-and-take of teacher and student that the teacher needs to master to be an effective player.

Why do I include "A Fourth Grade Dilemma"? Because it amuses me and because it works so well. Giving students forced choices doesn't necessarily create or solve any particular discipline problems, but using this is a fun part of effective gamesmanship and the overall craft of teaching.

Once you have had a funding of experience of discipline situations and problems you have personally handled, you will have the raw material with which to start thinking through your own philosophy of discipline. My comments on the philosophy of discipline may help you find your own place among some popular approaches to discipline.

I wait until near the end of this chapter to discuss reading levels and discipline problems because after I had otherwise begun to deal effectively with classroom discipline as a beginning teacher, it took me a long time to realize that most of my remaining problems were from students masking their own reading inadequacies. You should be alert to this etiology of so many school discipline problems.

I end the chapter with miscellaneous tips. After the playbook is set and the season is well under way, the best a coach can usually do is pass on a few timely tips.

All the components of this chapter emphasize minimizing discipline problems through effective curriculum planning and by having well-considered policies and procedures. Some discipline problems are inevitable, however. This chapter deliberately approaches what to do from a variety of perspectives. The key is to become more sophisticated and savvy in recognizing the nature of the problem and the variety of possible student and teacher responses. Having well-conceived expectations and procedures is an excellent place to start.

Expectations and Procedures

You must think through your expectations and procedures for each area of classroom behavior. These will be the areas where students test you most often. I think the following list is a great list, a comprehensive list that Ember, Evertson, Clements, Sanford, and Worsham (1981, Tables 2 & 3) compiled.[1] I've never found an expectation or policy that I have had or seen that isn't suggested by this list.

I will follow the list with my suggestions about my own choices and the pros and cons of my choices. The expectations and procedures have to fit an individual teacher's style, but thinking through the implications of the choices by contrasting your views with mine should help you find your own best policies and procedures.

Procedures for Classrooms

Procedures for Beginning Class

1. Administrative matters: The teacher needs procedures to handle reporting absences and tardiness. Students need to know what behaviors are expected of them while the teacher is completing administrative procedures. Some teachers begin the period with a brief warm-up exercise such as a few problems or a brief assignment. Others expect the students to sit quietly and wait for the teacher to complete the routine.

2. Student behavior before and at the beginning of the period: Procedures should be established for what students are expected to do

when the tardy bell rings (be in seats, stop talking), behavior during announcements (no talking, no interruptions of the teacher), what materials are expected to be brought to class each day, and how materials to be used during the period will be distributed.

*Procedures During Whole
Class Instructional Activities*

1. Student talk: Many teachers require that students raise their hands to receive permission to speak. Sometimes teachers allow chorus responses (everybody answers at once) without hand raising, but the teacher then needs to identify and use some signal to students that lets them know when such responding is appropriate.
2. Use of the room by students: Students should know when it is appropriate to use the pencil sharpener, when it is appropriate to obtain materials from shelves or bookcases, and if and when it is appropriate to leave their seats to seek help from the teacher or other students. Unclear expectations in this area result in some students spending time wandering about the room.
3. Leaving the room: Some procedures need to be established for allowing students to use the bathroom, go to the library or school office, and so on. Usually the school will have some specified system. Teachers who are free with hall passes frequently have large numbers of requests to leave the room.
4. Signals for attention: Teachers often use a verbal sign or a cue such as moving to a specific area of the room, ringing a bell, or turning on an overhead projector to signal to students. Such a signal, if used consistently, can be an effective device for making a transition between activities or for obtaining student attention.
5. Student behavior during seat work: Expectations need to be established for what kind of talk, if any, may occur during seat work, how students can get help, when out-of-seat behavior is or is not permitted, access to materials, and what to do if seat work assignments are completed early.
6. Procedures for laboratory work or individual projects: A system for distributing materials when these are used is essential. Also, safety routines or rules are vital. Expectations regarding appropriate behavior should be established for students working individually or in groups and when extensive movement around the room or coming and going is required. Finally, routines for cleaning up are suggested.

Expectations Regarding Student Responsibility for Work

1. Policy regarding the form of work: Procedures can be established for how students are to place headings on paper, for the use of pencil or pen, and for neatness.

2. Policy regarding completion of assignments: The teacher will have to decide whether incomplete or late work is acceptable, and under what conditions, and whether a penalty will be imposed. In addition, some procedure for informing students of due dates for assignments should be established, along with procedures for make-up work for students who are absent.

3. Communicating assignments to students: An effective procedure for communicating assignments is to keep a list of each period's work assignments during a 2- or 3-week period of time. Posting this list allows students who are absent to identify necessary make-up work easily. Another useful procedure is to record the assignment for the day on an overhead projector transparency or on the front chalkboard, and require students to copy the assignment onto a piece of paper or into a notebook. Students who do not complete assignments in class will then have a record of what is expected when they return to the assignment at home or during a study period.

4. Checking procedures: Work that is to be checked by students in class can save the teacher and provide quick feedback to students. Procedures should be established for exchanging papers, how errors are to be noted, and how papers are to be returned and passed to the teacher.

5. Grading policy: Students should know what components will be included in determining report card grades and the weight or percentage of each component.

Other Procedures

1. Student use of teacher desk or storage areas: Generally, these are kept off limits to students, except when the teacher gives special permission.

2. Fire and disaster drills: Students should be informed early in the year about what they are to do during emergencies. Typically, the school will have a master plan and will conduct schoolwide drills.

3. Procedures for ending the class: Expectations regarding straightening up the room, returning to seats, noise level, and a signal for dismissal may be established. When clean-up requires more than a

few seconds, teachers usually set aside the necessary time at the end of the period to complete the task before the bell rings.

4. Interruptions: Students need to know what is expected during interruptions (continue working or sit quietly).

Discussing the Basic Expectations

The above list is a great list. You need to consider your own need for policies in each and every area listed. A good exercise is to sit down with another teacher or teacher candidate and think through the range of possible expectations and procedures and the advantages and disadvantages of each choice. In this section, I suggest a range of such expectations and procedures and why I have the preferences that I have.

Beginning Class

1. Administrative matters: My research indicates that by the time students graduate from high school, they spend more time watching commercials (not programs, commercials) than they spend in instructional time. I hate to waste any part of my period. I want students engaged immediately. And I want an introductory activity that will settle them down while I take roll. The quickest way to raise doubts about your teaching effectiveness is for the attendance office to be complaining about not having attendance slips. This will worry a principal. Not only is attendance the way schools collect revenue, but if a student is cutting class, there's a huge chance the student is causing mischief somewhere.

In terms of taking roll, calling names takes too long and invites low-level discipline problems. I use a technique I call "negative attendance taking." Most students are in class even if you have a significant truancy problem. You do not need to know who is in class so much as who is not. It takes less time to figure out who is missing. If you subtract the number of students who are in class from the number of those on your roll, you know the number you have to mark absent. As it turns out, most of those will be the same students as those who were absent the day before. I don't mind asking the students sitting near me, "Who is missing?" They usually know. If they do not, that may indicate a student who may need special attention. In any instance, it is always quicker than calling roll, with many fewer attendant problems.

Figure 3.1. Discussing the basic expectations.

2. Behavior at the beginning of class: I try to post the opening assignment clearly on the board so that students know what to do immediately. I want them in their seats. I hate having students wandering around. I don't mind a bit of noise in my classroom, but I get uneasy with students up and about. Having said that, for me a student isn't officially tardy until I close the classroom door. If I am having a problem with one or two students being tardy, I will sometimes stand at the door when the bell rings, holding the door open, reminding any student within sight that when I close the door he or she will, indeed, be tardy. It is a part of gamesmanship. Catching as many students tardy as possible is not the game. . . .

I have a huge problem with announcements. If they are read over the public address system, students will not listen. Is the most important thing in your day making students listen to announcements? Yet, if the principal walks in and your students are talking or otherwise messing around, it looks bad. I cut a deal with my students. "The stuff in the announcements may be really important for you to hear. I can't make you know that. You can work on the opening assignment during this time, but you shouldn't talk because someone else may have their lives changed by something they hear . . ."

If it is up to me to read the announcements, I do a quick read. If you have sophomores, you can skip the announcements for the other classes. I will also take the liberty to highlight and post. By that, I mean I try to read the entire bulletin in less than 1 minute by saying the highlights: "Key Club meets Saturday, dance Friday, football game Tuesday, and I will post the bulletin in case you need the details." If someone asks a question, I answer it.

The issue of books and supplies is particularly difficult for me. I believe that one of my primary duties as an educator is to help students become more responsible. That entails bringing their books, paper, and pencil or pen to each and every class. That could become the only lesson plan for the year, however. Some students will forget. Are you willing to pay the price of a student who is unprepared being unable to participate for an entire period? Not me. It is too costly. If a student does not have the book, I will let him or her share with a neighbor. If a student does not have paper or pencil, he or she can ask a classmate to borrow such. And if the student has worn out all friendships, I have newsprint and pencil stubs. Students can always do their assignments with newsprint and pencil stubs, but they do not like it, and they are much more likely to bring their own supplies next time.

I tried with mixed success the idea of holding some possession of the student's ransom while he or she borrowed a pen from me. The student would give me something that I'd keep at my desk until he or she returned the pen. Too often, I was left with the billfold, student body card, belt, purse, or hairbrush instead of my pen.

During Whole Class Instruction

1. Student talk: I prided myself when I was a student on talking without ever raising my hand. It was much more fun to insert the telling point without having to have been recognized. I also know that when you do hand raising, someone will get left out who will be steamed! It is a matter of trade-offs. You do have some control if you have students raise their hands. But that isn't necessarily better for the conversation, and add that to the fact that you are probably being seen as having discriminated against someone with their hand up. This is such a problem for me that I have minimized full class discussions and become very fond of small group work, where it isn't such an issue.

2. Use of the room by students: I hate having students wander around the room. I will not have a pencil sharpener or drinking foun-

tain that works in my room. I remove the temptation. I'd rather be asked for a dictionary than wonder why someone is up and about. It is not that it never happens in my classroom, but it does as seldom as possible.

3. Leaving the room: The usual request to leave the classroom is to go to the bathroom. I've heard the stories of the teacher refusing to let a student go to the bathroom and the student urinating in the garbage can. Probably apocryphal, but maybe not. I remember that I tried to get permission to go to the bathroom every day in Latin. Such requests are more than likely a sign that the student is having problems with your curriculum. If you are getting a number of bathroom requests, you better pep up your curriculum.

In the meantime, what do you do? Frankly, a male teacher should be wary of ever telling a female student that she cannot go. The public citation of "feminine reasons" for such a request is a sure way of focusing the full class's attention on the teacher.

This is an area where I believe very strongly in NOT announcing your rules. My unannounced rule is that a student can go without question once in a term. The second time, I let the student go but tell that student, so that the whole class hears, that he or she needs to see me after class. After class, I tell the student that the quota is three. More than that requires a doctor's note that there is some kind of problem. I also query the student whether or not this is a matter of them being bored by my curriculum, and whether I can make changes that will improve their interest. If you announce that your quota is three, all your students will want to go each of the last three days of the term, and then what do you do?

Finally, I abhor the idea of carrying around a hub cap or some such hall pass to go to the restroom. I think that is demeaning. I know it works for some teachers, and their students do not seem to mind. I am not sure if this is a blind spot in my sense of humor. But I think it is demeaning to lug around a tire iron or hub cap or other conspicuous pass announcing to the world that I'm headed to the head. My idea about respecting students is that if they have to go that badly, I will interrupt the class and write them a pass. If you have a good curriculum, that interruption becomes its own disincentive to interrupt unless it truly is important to go.

4. Signals for attention: To my dismay, one of my strongest beginning teachers used a whistle to call for attention. I hated the idea. But it worked for her.

I think a key is to minimize the number of times you call for attention. Try to call for the full class's attention as seldom as possible. I have learned that if I forgot something, I should just wait and mention

Figure 3.2. Setting expectations and procedures for leaving the room.

it the next time I have the class' attention. It takes too much energy to command the attention of the full class. This is the kind of thing that wears a teacher out prematurely.

What are some other gestures to signal for attention? Raising your hand or moving to a particular spot in the classroom are two of the most common methods. Both are preferable to raising your voice. Teaching is something like running a marathon each day. You cannot unnecessarily waste energy. I like moving to a particular spot in the classroom. It tends to take a few more seconds to gain the class's attention, but it is less wearing.

5. Behavior during seat work: Your policies in this regard are clearly about advantages and disadvantages. I never assign seating. I never have a seating chart. One of the consequences is that during seat work, there is often a buzz in the classroom. That's the price I pay to avoid other consequences. My experience is that friends are going to talk to each other regardless. I hate them yelling at each other across the room. That bothers me a lot more than the buzz. Also, students can often solve a problem themselves if they can move. You may avoid an in-class fight by not having had a seating chart. After the first day, students usually sit in the exact same seat anyway. You will not have trouble taking roll because of this. And if a student moves, that is very interesting and may be worth asking about (privately).

I believe in Mike Myers' rule of vague directions (see his six rules, identified later in this chapter). Most students figure out what you expect immediately, and the others were not going to figure it out by you talking more. One of the best ways of having students get their questions answered effectively and efficiently is for them to ask their neighbor. You can handle the few remaining questions that students couldn't get answered in that way. Therefore, my policy is that students can talk quietly (and briefly) during seat work time to anyone contiguous to them. (It's also a vocabulary opportunity to discuss the meaning of *contiguous*.) If you can put up with the buzz, it will make your job much easier and students much happier.

6. Procedures for lab work and projects. One of my self-imposed cardinal rules is to teach what needs to be learned. For example, music groups are judged on poise. Music teachers should have lessons where no music is involved and the students work strictly on demeanor. If there are procedures for lab work or projects, make that part of your lesson plan.

In terms of group projects, I work a lot with small groups. I generally arrange the desks so that the groups that I want are prearranged. For example, if I want six groups of six, I adjust the rows so that the groups of six are self-evident. That helps a lot during transition time.

In regard to cleaning up, if it is a particularly messy day, I stroll through aisles with a garbage can in my hand. I don't say anything, just carry the can. Someone always objects that this is the custodian's job. I'm not bothered by this argument. By carrying the garbage can, I have established that I do not feel that cleaning up is beneath anyone, and it is a lot quicker than doing it all by myself at the end of the period.

Student Responsibility for Work

1. Form of work: I already think we spend too much time teaching conformity and compliant behavior. I will settle for the name on the paper. It's nice if the period and date are added, but I am not going to refuse work that comes in without it.

2. Completion of assignments. I have a huge problem with lowering the grade of a late assignment. In my mind, it is hard enough to give an accurate reading on the quality of academic work without adding behavioral issues. And I hate grading late work. If it is a good assignment, I have to get into a zone to do the grading. It requires a higher level of concentration, and I hate trying to get back into that zone. I'd rather not accept late work at all.

My personal solution requires me to avoid a strict point system of grading. As often as possible, a missed assignment is a missed opportunity. Except for a cumulative final exam, I have never felt that any other assignment is absolutely necessary. I have always felt that I could arrive at a fair overall grade on many fewer assignments than I would give over a semester.

Once you have given an exam, the questions are "out there." If you give an exam first period, by the time second period rolls around, some student knows something about that exam. Giving the same exam the next day or next week is silly. I advise never to give the same exam twice. So what do you do if you have to give a make-up exam? As often as possible, make the make-up exam a long essay exam. The student will usually earn a comparable grade to the other work in the class, and long essays are never seen as easier alternatives to having attended the regular exam.

I also have a public policy on due dates for papers. I set a date that papers are due. I set a past due date of a few days later. No papers will be accepted after the past due date. I say that on the first day of class, each student should go to the post office immediately and buy stamps and an envelope that will hold a paper. I announce that I will accept any paper that has a postmark of the past due date or before. That way, even if a student is in the hospital being fed by IVs, someone can mail his or her term paper. Do these policies work 100%? Of course not. But they do minimize the exceptions greatly.

By the way, the usual standard is that students get an extra day for each day they were absent to make up their work. Although this is a good standard, it does not necessarily reflect how much time it will take a student to keep up and make up at the same time.

3. Communicating assignments: Encourage students to call each other if they are absent to clarify assignments. Post all assignments clearly on the board and leave them there as long as necessary. (And be sure to write "Do Not Erase" on your blackboard.) It is also a good idea to keep a notebook of assignments for the term so that anyone can go back and see what has been expected. One of your students might be willing to keep this notebook up to date.

4. Checking procedures: DO NOT HAVE STUDENTS GRADE EITHER THEIR OWN WORK OR EACH OTHER'S WORK. Regardless of the timeliness or efficiency of doing this, it communicates that you did not think the work important. And if you collect it, I guarantee someone will fudge the results.

I have found a fairly effective way of marking those assignments that you want done but aren't sure deserve a grade per se. I mark such assignments with something that approximates the A, B, C grading scale without having that stigma. If something is excellent, I mark a plus; good, a check-plus; okay, a check; and poor, a minus. Students do not complain so much about the mark as they would about an A, B, C, or D. I also tell students that if they have a pattern of pluses, I weigh it into their overall grade.

A final tip: I have found that an excellent assignment is to ask students to write their 10 best questions about what we are studying, promising them that they will NOT have to answer those questions. Questions 3-8 are usually great indicators of how students are managing the material. I mark these papers by circling the number of the questions that I think are the best questions.

5. Grading policy: I am a firm believer that the system is meant to serve the students and that the teacher is the final judge of the quality of work. Point systems are too often arbitrary and capricious. Who should be in the hall of fame? Some baseball players make it for short, brilliant careers. Others make it for long if less distinguished careers. Who deserves an A? In my mind, the brilliant student who has great papers and tests along with the student who has consistently strong performances over all the coursework.

I am also a strong believer in the cumulative final. I have a teacher friend who was in a fight with a student, a literal fight. This student had known for some time that he could not possibly pass even though there were weeks left in the term. Quite frankly, I am not willing to have a student in my class who doesn't have a chance to pass the class through the final exam. And it isn't only because I don't want that student to put sugar in my gas tank. If that student can pass my cumulative final, he or she has learned enough not to repeat the class. After all, a D-, D, D+, or C- do not recommend the student for graduation. If you cannot be on the side of the student up to and during the final exam, you are in a lot of trouble.

As far as tendencies go, I tend to be seen as too hard on the grade of A and too easy on the grade of B. I am not apologetic for this tendency. Those earning an A should be preparing themselves for college. You want them to be successful when they get there. In regard to the grade of B, it is not a recommendation for an exclusive college. Students can get into the state college and community college systems with lower grades than that. And if you are an effective teacher, more effective than most, wouldn't you think most of your students will have been sufficiently inspired to earn at least a B?

That doesn't mean that I don't give Cs. But in a sense, the C student will know that he or she earned that lower grade. I hate Ds. It is hard to accept them as anything less than an insult. A C- will do the same thing. The student will have to earn a higher grade somewhere else to graduate with a 2.0 average. I rarely have Fs, although an occasional student will surprisingly demand one, usually so he or she can wreak some vengeance on his or her family.

Other Procedures

1. Student use of teacher desk or storage areas: Off limits! Period! And you need to keep your grade book under lock and key. Even better, make periodic copies. I knew a science teacher who had her car stolen with her grade book in the car. Nightmare! Major nightmare!

2. Fire and disaster drills: I am something of a nonconformist. I hate lines. Especially at the high school level, making young adults walk in lines like elementary school students is awkward at best. But you cannot afford to be embarrassed by your students during a fire drill. If the students need to know it, teach it. I practice fire drills before the school fire drill. I want an agreement with students. I won't make them walk in a straight line if they will walk in a group, quietly, close enough to me that they can hear me speak in a normal tone of voice, to the designated fire area. This is risky, but so is trying to take them to the designated area in a straight line. Things can fall apart very quickly for the new teacher, and this will be the one time your whole class is on public display.

3. Ending class: If students are lining up at your door before the bell rings, you are in trouble. The reason I advocate a third activity for each class period is to make sure something constructive is happening up until the bell. NEVER use the end of the period to work on homework! Only a supernerd does homework then. Others start getting more and more restless.

If the bell is about to ring, accept defeat, do NOT try to intercept the class at the door. If the bell is not about to ring, you can go to the door, stand vigilantly in front of it, and insist that all students return to their desks before you release them from their obligations. This will restore a certain amount of order, but the next day you need something in your curriculum to keep students meaningfully occupied until the end of class. You can anticipate this problem by reacting to the kids zipping up their backpacks. "We aren't done . . . but if you weren't distracting me with your packing, I could be done before next period starts." Ha!

4. Interruptions: Once you have your class more or less under control, you should have a heart-to-heart talk about not embarrassing each other. Promise to make every attempt to discipline privately, and call the parent or guardian of the student's selection only if there is a problem. You, in turn, need for students to protect you when there is an interruption and/or visitor. They should keep working, and work quietly. In turn, you will be their champion should they get into hot water somewhere else. . . .

In conclusion, I have tried to describe my considerations and the pros and cons of my choices. Start with the premise that a policy, any policy, has built-in advantages and disadvantages. The only surety is that what has worked for me will not work exactly for you. But the better you think through each of these areas, the fewer discipline problems you will have.

∼ Mike Myers' Six Rules for More Savvy Teaching

Ninety-nine percent of the time I have spent in inservice training has been of limited use (and too often boring). When I heard Mike Myers talk, I found myself not only paying attention but taking notes. Not only did he share a magnificent list of six rules, but he shared it with the sense of good humor and goodwill that is all too often in short supply.[2]

1. The rule of secondary side effects: This rule acknowledges that curricular choices have important side effects. A worksheet will not only provide students opportunities to learn their subject matter, it will also serve as a mantra, soothing nerves and calming students.

2. The rule of vague directions: Make your directions vague and don't repeat them. Most students will figure out what to do anyway, and the others will need special, individual help anyway. (The alternative is to have 30 students ask you the same question 30 times.)

3. The rule of frames: Whatever you assign, some students will want to do something else. Your response: "No, you don't have to do this, but you'll have to make individual arrangements with me. No, not now. After class."

4. The rule of shared authority: To understand this rule, announce to your class that Adolf Hitler was the 33rd president of the United States. If you're lucky, one student in class will question whether this is true. Your point is that you don't have to be the expert on everything, and students better bring something to class that they know, too.

5. The rule of procedural specificity: A good example of this rule is instructing students to put their names and period number in the top right-hand corner of their papers. This lets students know that this is a serious, important assignment. To not do so signals to students it is not important.

6. The rule of pretense: For students to have some prospect of being successful, you must communicate to them that "they can already

do this." "We are just going to practice it so you do it better." Whether it's true or not.

An Addendum

Homework is a cultural statement. Whether your students plan on doing any homework or not, they expect to be assigned some. It tells them you care about them. It tells them what you are expecting of them is important. It offers them the camaraderie of facing your unrealistic expectations together.

So Now What Do I Do?
Physical Ploys to Affect Student Behavior

The classroom is getting a little out of hand? You need a wide repertoire of possible responses. The more variety, the better the likelihood of success. Even if you learn by heart and practice religiously every idea presented in this book, you will have periodic breakdowns in discipline. So now what do you do? Well, the trick that worked today won't necessarily work again tomorrow. You have to diversify your reactions and keep students guessing. With that in mind, I tried to think of everything I had ever done to gain students' attention and curb their errant behavior. Most of these acts can be practiced in a mirror. It is good to review the list periodically to see if you haven't been overdoing the same technique and underusing some other perfectly good ones. I will emphasize yet again that they work best when portrayed dramatically, but on a base of goodwill and good humor.

Facial Expressions

- Look askance
- Stare
- Glower
- Frown—lick lips (and shake head)
- Flare nostrils
- Widen eyes (in wrath)
- Grimace

Figure 3.3. Physical Ploys to Affect Student Behavior.

- Raise an eyebrow
- Give the evil eye (one severely raised eyebrow)
- Look disgusted
- Make an angry face
- Make a funny face

More Physical Responses

- Choke student (a student who likes you, done with humor)
- Look at your watch
- Hang on the desk
- Move into student's physical space
- Touch a student's arm
- Take a student by arm (near the biceps)
- Intimidate physically (loom and glower)

- Shake head in disgust
- Hit fist into palm
- Hold hands together as if in prayer
- Have a predetermined gesture (e.g., holding index finger up) to ask for silence
- Whistle
- Blow a whistle
- Grit teeth
- Clench fists
- Hit forehead with hand
- Be perfectly quiet
- Shrug shoulders
- Point at student
- Wag finger
- Give "cut" sign with hand
- Raise arms for quiet
- Stamp foot
- Clap hands
- Put hands on face
- Snap fingers
- Make a face
- Gnash teeth
- Give umpire's "out of there" sign with thumb
- Give thumbs-down motion

Use Your Voice

- Yell, scream, shout
- "Hey!"
- Give specific behavioral direction
- Whisper
- Badger
- Insist verbally
- Use irony
- Tell students trying to help you that you don't need help
- "Tsk, tsk"

- Ask a student to stop specific behavior
- Threaten to move the student
- Threaten to call the student's home
- Give a (loving) tongue lashing
- Bargain/negotiate
- Insult (tongue in cheek)
- Raise voice
- Joke
- Don't argue
- Talk about the student out loud to others (about something else, it's a distraction)
- Have the class give the student its attention
- Have the class point at a student (only with humor)
- Call the student's name
- Call the student's name in another context
- Call the student's middle name without looking at him or her
- Mention something the student is knowingly interested in
- Scold
- Sigh
- Grunt
- Scoff
- Plead
- Warn
- Offer commentary on the student's behavior (like a sports commentator)
- Praise mightily for something the student does well, something obviously unrelated to the current issue
- Clear throat
- Cough
- Poke fun
- Threaten to break thumbs
- Laugh
- Say, in an off-the-wall fashion, "No one said you had to pass my class"
- Say, in an off-the-wall fashion to someone obviously passing your class, "There's still a chance you could pass my class"
- Say "That's an F for the day," as if you kept such records

Feints

- Ask if a move of seats would be salutary
- Use the guilt squeeze
- Ignore
- Talk without looking
- Don't put a student's name on the board; that's too elementary
- Don't place a student in the corner, that garners too much attention
- Change the subject or activity
- Divert attention
- Turn off the lights
- Pretend you are having a heart attack

Actions, Responses, Adjustments

- Talk to the student privately
- Talk to the student just outside the door
- Talk to the student after class
- Call the student's home
- Make a behavior contract with the student
- Threaten to take away points (I'm not for doing this)
- Give detention (I'm not for punishing the teacher, so I don't like this)
- Ask another student you both like to talk to the student
- Give the student a contingency: Do this or that
- Don't do activities students cannot handle
- Tape the noise of the class and play it back
- Call the student to your desk
- Move (you or the student)
- Send the student to the library (but have an agreement with the librarian)
- Send the student to another teacher (again, with prior agreement)
- Flick the lights for attention
- Send the student outside the classroom door to be spoken to at the first reasonable opportunity

- Call the parent or guardian at work
- Make an assignment
- Give the student a puzzle or maze to solve quietly
- Go to your desk drawer, as if to pull out a referral or detention slip
- Pull out the referral or detention slip (with a flare)
- Take a trash can to the student (especially for forbidden gum)
- Ask other students to help by not reinforcing this student's misbehavior (this usually means to ignore the student when he or she is acting out)
- Send the student to the counselor
- Send the student to the vice principal (very last resort)
- Call the student's home
- Assign a good deed
- Write the student a short, to the point, note
- Send a letter home
- Bribe the student
- Ask a littering student to pick up 10 pieces of litter
- Assign a worksheet
- Go over the grade book with the student
- Give a test
- Withhold a privilege
- Put on a mask or funny face
- Go on strike (assignments only, no teaching)
- Change the activity
- Use a diversion (pick a foil, a student who is safe to pick on whom you like a lot, to elicit a behavior you are more concerned others in the class need to exhibit)
- Have other students point at the student and then ask, "Do you get the point?"
- Stand on your desk or chair

Action—Punishment

- Class detention
- Office detention
- Referral to office
- Suspension

Of course, you can use any of these moves in combinations. The key is to realize how many possibilities are at your disposal and not to rely too much on any one method.

20 Classic Teaching Mistakes

Once you recognize these mistakes, it may drive you to distraction how often you unintentionally make them. But if you cut down the number of such mistakes, you should be that much happier.

For too many years, I sat in small desks that, by the way, are no more comfortable for students than they would be for you, and watched teachers make the same mistakes over and over again. So, I sat down at my typewriter (precomputer) and listed them all. I still make these mistakes, too, from time to time—but I wish I didn't, and I try not to.

In baseball, if the right fielder drops a fly ball, he gets an error—E-9. But if he misses the cut-off man and a runner takes an extra base, the mistake never shows up in the box score as an official error. Below, I identify 20 teaching mistakes akin to missing the cut-off person. The items on this list are so commonplace that they would not likely be considered serious errors. They can still lead to losing the game, however.

1. Guess What's in My Mind

As a student, this one drives me nuts. Recently I heard a renowned educational speaker break from his lecture by asking questions and taking answers from his audience. I liked the idea of asking us questions, only really what we were supposed to do was guess what was already in his mind. He asked us the three fears people had that kept them from succeeding at computers. The moment I heard him use the word "three," I knew he didn't really want to hear our answers. I, myself, knew there were really four reasons, not three. More venturesome members of the audience played along and gave their own ideas. The speaker then deftly reinterpreted the responses into his three answers. He was playing "guess what's in my mind." When the audience didn't guess too well, he told us the three reasons.

I consider this game dishonest. If you ask a question, you should care about the person's answer. The best questions (unless reviewing for a test) are those the speaker does not have a definitive answer to. If you find yourself asking others to guess what's in your mind, the most obvious thing to do is to tell your audience to guess what's in your mind or to give them the answer and move on.

2. Poll Taking

Virtually every teacher I have observed makes this mistake frequently. They ask "Does everyone understand?" or "Can we go on?" or "Do you remember that?" Three "smacks"—who always nod their heads affirmatively—nod their heads affirmatively, and the teacher assumes these three speak for the entire class and continues. If you want accurate class feedback to an important question, you should take a quick, but accurate, person-by-person poll.

3. Competing With Self

This mistake is almost as ubiquitous as the previous two. Its most frequent manifestation is that the teacher has already passed out the worksheet and now he or she is trying to make some unrelated point to the class. A variation is passing materials throughout the class to see and touch while trying to lecture on said materials. A classic case I recently saw was a music teacher passing musical instruments around the class while trying to lecture on the different kinds of instruments. Don't compete with yourself by trying to talk over something else you have caused the class to attend to. It wastes energy and causes frustration.

4. Arguing With Kids

Don't argue with kids. Especially in front of the class. I observed an English teacher pass out an article. One precocious student complained about the arbitrariness of the article. The teacher got into a prolonged argument with the kid. On one level, the teacher won the argument. The student acquiesced. But the other students watched with some frustration as the teacher sank to their level. In private, you can have honest discussions with students, but arguments in front of the class harm the integrity of the professional role. "Let's talk about it after class" is a much safer out.

Figure 3.4. I have never found a "safe" discipline problem when confronting a student in front of his or her peers.

5. Disciplining a Student in Front of Peers

I have never had a student who was a discipline problem when confronted alone. I have never found a "safe" discipline problem when confronting a student in front of his or her peers. My rule is, divide and conquer. How I follow that rule usually is to ask a student to step outside so that we can discuss his or her issue privately as soon as the class is in a situation that will allow me to step outside, too. Outside, I have always found students willing to be reasonable, even contrite. Inside, students have to play to their audience. Don't put them in that predicament of being cornered.

There is an almost unbelievable difference in handling a discipline problem in front of the class, or privately, one-on-one. A student who may be defiant if disciplined in front of the class will almost always be contrite when dealt with privately. If you have truly cultivated your ability to appreciate each student for the strategies he or she is trying to both implement and adapt to get through life, always start your private conversation with the whole truth. Be honest, but find the larger truth first. Your comments might go something like this, "You know I like having you in class. You know I like your energy. You know that you are having success in my class. This is only about your interrupting the class. I need (specify) this from you."

6. Apologizing

Don't ever apologize. I mean, don't ever make excuses in front of the class. "I forgot the worksheet." "I couldn't get the movie projector." "I wish I'd had more time for this." Regardless of your sincere intent, students hear you as being defensive about being ill-prepared. And ill-prepared means unprofessional. Brazen it out. The lesson may very well work anyway. Lessons with everything well planned often fail for whatever reason, and you are stuck with the blame. Sometimes the lessons with missing components work for no explicable reason. So don't apologize, justify, or defend. There is no use making things even worse.

7. No Wait Time After Questions

I think every teacher makes this mistake every class. Teachers almost never wait even 3 seconds when there is a pause after a question. Even a 3-second pause will yield better, more thoughtful student responses. But teachers don't wait. If there's a pause, they answer the question themselves, or ask yet another question even less likely to generate a good answer. It's okay to wait at least 10 seconds so students learn you are serious about soliciting good answers.

8. Not Circulating Throughout the Class During Seat Work

I know why teachers don't circulate much during seat work and why they don't like to do so. Often teachers give students seat work so they can get a rest. And they often also don't like the hassle of personally encountering students who aren't doing the assignment or aren't doing it very well. But such reluctance to circulate is always short-sighted. The student not doing the assignment while the teacher is buried at the teacher's desk creates discipline problems increasingly difficult to handle. The students who do the work wrong from the start take even more teacher time to straighten out. In 60 seconds, you can monitor the entire class. Entering each student's space tends to get them on-task, at least for the moment. And short, friendly words or clarification or encouragement are often worth more than 50 minutes of directions to the whole class.

9. Inappropriate Expectations

The tendency is to overestimate what students can do when you get them at the beginning of the school year but to underestimate how much progress they can make in a term or a year with you. High expectations tend to be correlated with high achievement. I am impressed that excellent teachers set high goals. But many of these same teachers try to start with students at too high a level. Students need to be successful early to reach high standards later.

10. Attention Reinforces Negative Behavior

I thought about this a lot one summer when my in-law's dog was locked up in a side yard while my young daughter swam. The dog tended to knock kids over. The dog managed to get out after we had gone into the house. He made a beeline for the slightly open patio door, only to bump harshly into the screen door. My mother-in-law, legitimately concerned about the longevity of her screen door, yelled at the dog and went outside to catch him. She managed to chase him, but not catch him, as he dashed about barking eagerly. Finally, my mother-in-law went back inside, only to hear the dog rush once more eagerly into the screen door. Once again he got a similar reaction. My mother-in-law yelled and gave chase. Her intent in yelling and chasing was to sanction the dog's behavior. By the time this scenario had happened a fourth time, it became apparent the dog loved the scolding and chase. Very often, the class disturber gets the attention he or she seeks, thus reinforcing rather than extinguishing the behavior. Ignoring the negative behavior and reinforcing other constructive behaviors works more effectively.

11. Teaching Stuff You Wouldn't Learn

One of my student teachers, who was struggling with a difficult class, was, among other things, trying to teach her ninth-grade students relative pronouns. I have a PhD from an accredited university, and I have to look relative pronouns up to make sure I remember what they are. So should they be taught to ninth graders? I'm reluctant to teach material I never found sufficiently important to have ever learned.

12. Writing Test Items That Are Easily Written Rather Than Measuring What Was Actually Taught

Although I generally use essay tests, I recently wrote an hour's worth of multiple choice items for a 2-hour college final for an educational psychology course. We had spent about 20% of our time on evaluation. But I had so much fun writing evaluation questions (which turned out to be the easiest items for me to write) that they ended up being 33% of my list of final questions. I reduced the worth of each of the evaluation questions to bring them more in line with the emphasis I had given them in class. One of the reasons I am so conscientious is in deference to the many inane and, to my mind, unfair tests I took in school that ironically led me to pursue a career in education.

13. Ironclad Point Standards for Grades

I recently had a student tell me she had missed an A by half a point. Her C on the very first test of the term, followed by a B and then all As, had cost her an A. The teacher lamented with her that she had missed an A by so little. That's CRAP! The teacher decides what grade goes on the report card. Evaluation is an inexact science. The statistical concepts of true scores and of standard error of measure give us tools that allow us *confidence bands* instead of arbitrary distinctions such as 70-C, 80-B, 90-A. Students deserve the benefit of the doubt. One test that's anomalous may reflect more about the test than the student. To tell a student he or she missed an A by half a point is simply wrong. You can review the student's work and consider it B or A work, but it is wrong to blame the lower grade on a half a point.

14. Overcalling the Name of a Student You Are Worried About

I recently observed a truly exceptional PE class, but this near flawless teacher called one name, Anthony, more than twice the times any student's name was called. In my opinion, this student's behavior did not warrant so much name calling. But if the self-fulfilling prophecy becomes operative here, Anthony is much more likely to confirm the teacher's expectation and misbehave. Just this past term, I found myself calling on one particular student too often. I realized I had expected some problems from this student and had in fact invited rather than discouraged interruptions through my "preferential" treatment.

15. Bias in Grading Tests With Names on Them

In my undergraduate days, I saw a classmate in my freshman year get typified as an A student. From freshman year to senior year, I knew that she would get a higher grade in every class until qualifying exams at the end of the 4-year period, which would be the first exam graded anonymously. I felt vindicated when on this one anonymous test, I received a higher grade. Given all our petty biases and prejudices about race, sex, religion, size, age, party affiliation, and so on, I think it necessary to grade academic work anonymously.

16. Taking Things Personally

One of the radical ideas in the Postman and Weingartner (1969) book, *Teaching as a Subversive Activity,* is that teachers be required to teach outside their specialty. Such a practice helps alleviate the problem of taking things too personally. Teachers have a credential that proves they are highly invested in their subject matter. But by design, the overwhelming majority of students will not share a similar interest. Kids intuitively know that school is not only for learning, but for sorting and selection. Even most of the kids who elect to take music won't go on to become musicians. So the career music teacher with a passion for his or her field will inevitably be frustrated by both cavalier and callous attitudes toward his or her specialty. Just remember—it ain't personal. Invoke the serenity prayer: God help me to change the things I can; accept the things I can't; and have the wisdom to know the difference.

17. Red Ink

Who decided to use red ink? James Herndon knows. It was NoMan. Red ink is as indigenous to teaching as unreadable prescriptions are to medical doctors. And like unreadable prescriptions, red ink is dangerous. All the research I've seen indicates students learn better with encouragement; red ink is discouraging. I like a fellow teacher and neighbor's bumper sticker: "Find the good and praise it." I am indebted to Al Grommon, a former professor of mine and former president of the National Teachers of English. He taught us to write comments in pencil so we could erase them if we found we'd been harsh instead of constructive.

18. Threats

Many, if not most, books on discipline recommend making conditional statements to students. "If you don't _____, then I'll _____." Fill in the blanks. I'm troubled by that approach for two reasons. First, too many teachers learn to make the threat but don't follow through. Slow death. Second, as soon as you say, "If you don't sit down, I'm going to send you to the principal," you've backed yourself up against a wall. Now you have to send the kid to the office or lose face. It's a no-win situation. If the kid is crossing you, you should be clear with the kid that he or she is crossing you. Those few times a kid passed my line, especially my first year of teaching, I strode sternly to my desk and opened the drawer abruptly. From my drawn desk drawer, I took a pass, and I would prepare to send a kid to the library, another teacher (by previous arrangement and agreement), the counselor, or the dean. 'Tweren't no business but my own where I was prepared to send the student. With the good drama I had created, I would observe the student's response and decide how far the student had crossed the line and what was fair on my part and what I wanted to do. Or as Teddy Roosevelt used to say, "Speak softly and carry a big stick." No threats.

19. Asking, "Why Are You Doing This?"

I am amazed how many teachers ask students, "Why are you doing that?" Haven't teachers read *Mad Magazine's* snappy answers to stupid questions? Why did you hit Sam? Why did you pass that note? What do you think you are doing? Dumb questions! They invite answers. "I hit Sam because he has an ugly wart on his nose." "I passed the note because I need a date." "I'm trying to stay awake in class." Each answer may be true, so you can't get the kid in further trouble. Deal with the behavior, not the why.

20. Being Perfect

I do a rather elaborate oral interpretation of Edgar Allen Poe's "Telltale Heart." It's quite popular with some students. My second year of teaching, I was asked to do an encore performance after school. I said I would, but everyone needed to be on time. A few minutes past "on time," I locked my doors and started my presentation. After a while, a student started banging on the door to be let in. I just read louder. He knocked louder. By the end of the story, it wasn't clear who was louder, me reading about the beating of the hideous heart or the student pounding on the door. Exceedingly angry, I threw open the door (quote the Raven, "nevermore") and gave an unmerciful tongue lashing to the student. Humiliated both of us in front of all the others. Ironically, it eventually worked out for the best. I had made such a grievous error of judgment. I had a lot to be sorry for the next day, regardless of how the student felt about how he'd acted toward me. Without expectations of any apology from him, I sincerely apologized for my behavior. It was the bridge necessary for him, too, as it turned out. I don't encourage deliberate mistakes. But I've found accepting that I'll make mistakes, and the consequent responsibility for them, to be invaluable in making contact with students.

Classroom Games and How to Play Them

I consider the following to be the best, most insightful piece I've ever written. Once you realize the nature of these student ploys and start recognizing them and responding in kind, you will probably feel like you have an unfair advantage, and an extra sense. This section is reprinted courtesy of *High School Journal*.[3]

More often than not when you feel like tearing your hair out, you should actually laugh. More often than not, students are playing a well-rehearsed routine on you. If you recognize the game (and how can you have forgotten having played them yourself where you were a student?), you can laugh and move on. This is a good essay for when you are starting to take it all a bit too seriously. Even the most irritating behavior by students usually has a thinly disguised purpose. Just like it was when you were a kid.

I have been observing classrooms professionally for over 30 years. My experience has enabled me to identify a variety of games students play in the classroom. These games students play reflect the four "hidden agenda" items students have: Students expect to have something in class interest them; students generally don't want to work any harder than they can help; students want to gain attention; and students want to know each teacher's limits. It is surprising how many teachers fail to recognize the thrust of these games; undoubtedly they themselves played these same games as students.

Recognizing and understanding these games is essential for teachers who want to manage their classrooms effectively and maintain their sanity. As professor of secondary education at Pepperdine, I encourage my student teachers to enjoy the games their students will play, and, when called on to participate, to play well.

The "What Was It Like When You Were a Kid?" game is clearly diversionary. The students don't really care what it was like in the old days. The purpose is to change the subject, and if the teacher doesn't have a lesson that's working, the teacher often plays along with the graphic stories of how out-of-date everything was in "the golden age."

If the teacher can't keep the students interested in anecdotes, then the students are likely to create a more complicated game to alleviate boredom. On bus trips, it's "100 Bottles of Beer on the Wall." You surely remember—"99 bottles of beer on the wall, 99 bottles of beer, take one down, pass it around, 98 bottles of beer on the wall." It's the perfect game. The teacher is unlikely to break it up because at least the students are occupied and not tearing up the bus. The students like it because they shouldn't be singing about beer and because they know it is likely to drive the teacher and bus driver nuts with its repetitiveness.

In the classroom, similar games are varyingly obtrusive or unobtrusive. Two obtrusive ones are coughing at the same time and dropping books or pencils at the same time. More unobtrusive ones include counting the teacher's "uhs," racing pill bugs across floor tiles, passing notes, and writing dirty words on the desks. All variations of the game are relatively harmless; in fact, they are usually coping strategies to alleviate boredom. Or, as a student announced in my reading class one hot, tedious day, "Time really flies when you are having fun."

Slightly more serious, but also more animated, contentious, and fraught with drama and comedy are the games that revolve around students' desire to minimize both the workload and the teacher's high expectations. My favorite to watch is a variation of the more benign of the "Master/Servant" routines. It generally occurs when the teacher makes a new assignment. Some students throw up their hands; some throw their heads down on their desks; some threaten to throw up.

Figure 3.5. The Game: "Do My Work For Me."

They also groan and feign righteous indignation (I always expect one to threaten to call an attorney): "No, Sir, tell me it's not true. Sir, Sir, please don't make me do it, Sir." Of course the best response by the teacher is to laugh at the great performances and then to get clear with students the expectation that will govern the class.

A game with similar intention is the "Do My Work for Me" game. The teacher initiates the game by giving directions, usually on an assignment. The students make the subsequent moves: Individually—but really en masse—they ask the same questions over and over again. Students find this game to be effective in (a) getting the teacher to explain what has to be done in such detail that the students need not think for themselves, and (b) convincing the teacher of the need to lower his or her expectations of what is reasonable for the student to do. In playing this game, I advise the teacher to give the directions one time and to make those directions appropriately vague. The teacher should offer to answer questions individually, and then should proctor the classroom to see that each student actually ends up following the directions correctly.

A similar game is "They Never Learned Us That Before." Every year students swear they've never had nouns, verbs, adjectives, and adverbs. And every year the new teacher decides, Well, then, I'll teach it to them. This game assures students that they will not have to learn too much new material.

The final variation of this game is "It's Not My Fault." My creative writing students' talent for excuses was extraordinary—It fell into a mud puddle; my dog ate it; my mother made me take her to the doctor; I turned it in already; You (the teacher) must have lost it. This game, like the others, is designed to get students out of as much work as possible. The teacher's job is to recognize this pressure. The teacher should accept that students have the right to a reasonable workload, but the teacher must remind students that high teacher expectations correlate with high student achievement.

The third set of games includes both "Horshak" and "Pin the Tail on the Donkey." You have probably seen or heard of Arnold Horshak from the television show, *Welcome Back Kotter*. Horshak was, of course, the only sweathog in Mr. Kotter's special class who had internalized the hidden curriculum from the larger comprehensive school. When Mr. Kotter asked a "schoolish" question, Horshak would respond by waving his arm frantically and going, "ooh, ooh, ooh!" This was obviously "uncool," but Horshak had internalized the lessons Philip Jackson (1968) describes in *Life in Classrooms*: (a) students learn, or try to learn, so they will stand out in the "crowd" of the classroom; (b) students learn to respond in class in such a way as to receive teacher attention and praise; and (c) students learn to accept the unquestioned power of the teacher. So Horshak, whether or not he knew the answer to the question, always wanted to be recognized by Mr. Kotter. The competitiveness and eagerness with which students answer innocuous teacher questions is a good measure of how "on the school treadmill" a class is. This attitude also explains why some students so eagerly wave their hands to respond to a question, then ask to have the question repeated or admit they don't know the answer, or give a stupid answer. They often don't have an investment in the question: They are merely playing power, praise, and crowds—as I prefer to call it, Horshak. My response to the universality of this game is to promote more small group discussions, where the questions and answers are not so dependent on teacher attention.

Another powerful social game in the classroom—but one that involves the teacher less personally—is "Pin the Tail on the Donkey." This game has other names, including "Rating," "Ranking," and "Playing the Totem Pole." Students in every class are busy determining the pecking order and then protecting their place in that order. Student conflicts are often generated when two students have a serious disagreement over their relative positions in the order of things. Although these rankings are a necessary part of peer group interactions, they are usually impervious to teacher perception and intervention. Teachers will, however, see the signs of this game because it is merely a variation of scapegoating. The student's social position is automatically improved when someone else is humiliated in the classroom and falls, even if temporarily, to the bottom of the totem pole. This humiliation is akin to what has been dubbed the essential cultural nightmare: fear of failure/envy of success.

When I took beginning French in high school, my French teacher humiliated me in front of the class. She was telling me in French to write my name on the board. I had no idea what she was trying to get me to do, but she kept saying, "Michelle" over and over again. So I wrote "Michelle" on the board. She wasn't, however, asking me to write the feminine form on the board; she wanted me to write my name, Michael, in French, which is spelled and pronounced "Michel." When I wrote my name as "Michelle," the entire class had a good laugh at my expense, and I proceeded to drop out of sight as a respectable foreign language student. The teacher's responsibility in this game is to protect every potential donkey, and to minimize the catastrophes of public classroom humiliation and failures.

My final group of games revolves directly around the issue of teacher power. One of the most consternating is "This Class Is Boring" or its twin, "Gee, You're Mean." A student makes the public pronouncement to gauge the teacher's response. If the teacher responds to either charge with heated wrath, the students classify the teacher as an autocrat at best and a fascist at worst, and they will not make such charges very often. If the teacher responds with mild irritation, the students decide that the teacher is unsure of his or her professional role. If the teacher responds defensively, the students know the teacher cares but may also be vulnerable, a bit disorganized, and perhaps an easy touch. If the teacher responds, "Yes, mean and getting meaner," the students know they have their match in a secure teacher who expects a lot but most likely also cares how the students are doing as people.

Figure 3.6. The Game: "Gee, You're Mean."

~ A Fourth Grade Dilemma, A Trick of the Trade

It is almost unbelievable how well this works. It is almost like magic.

Okay already. I admit I'm about to tell a gross joke. But it's a fourth-grade classic and illustrates a central educational principle. So here it goes. Fourth grade. One kid asks the other, "What would you rather do: Slide down a 10-foot razor blade edge or . . . swim through a river of snot?" What's always most amazing about the question is that the other kid invariably answers, "Swim through a river of snot." Always. The kid asked the question never refuses to answer. And he or she always answers the nonlethal alternative—swim through the river of snot. Gross. But the implicit educational principle is classic. Give kids two choices and they will willingly choose the least horrible alternative; instead of despising you for offering them such choices, they will appreciate your magnanimity in giving them a choice.

Figure 3.7. A Fourth Grade Dilemma.

Would you rather have the test Thursday or Friday? Would you rather read Shakespeare's *The Tempest* or *Romeo and Juliet*? Would you rather have two essay questions on the test or one? Would you rather have one test or two? Would you rather have me lecture or you give your oral reports? Would you rather listen to the bulletin or have me scrape my nail on the blackboard? Would you like to have an extra test or a term paper? Would you rather complete the assignment or visit the dean? Would you like me to call your mother or your father about your misbehavior? Would you like detention, or to write 1,000 times "I LOVE MY TEACHER"? Would you like to get to work now or work through recess? Would you like to raise your hand before talking or have me break your arm? I mean really, what would you rather do: Slide down a 10-foot razor blade edge, or . . . swim through a river of snot?

Comments on the Philosophy of Discipline

Four works continue to influence my ideas about discipline. Alas, Jenny Gray's (1969) *The Teacher's Survival Guide* is long out of print. Her books were incredibly helpful to me as a starting teacher. She offers good advice and wisdom:

> Their protestations to the contrary notwithstanding, the need of young people for control, guidance, and protection from their own folly is as real as their need for food and sleep. Teacher popularity polls beyond number indicate that students reserve their highest accolades for the teacher who, ignoring good-natured taunts and complaints, maintains the steady pressure required to get the best behavior and the best work from them. New teachers invariably react with surprise when they discover for the first time that the vast majority of young people prefer firmly controlled, well-planned classes. A picnic atmosphere is fun for a while, but it soon palls for all but the farthest-out young patrons. (p. 94)

Exactly! Thus she warns that, "some individuals are too kind, too sympathetic, too peace-loving ever to make very effective teachers." Ha! I am not surprised that Gray (1969) reports receiving "a number of indignant letters" about her being cynical about kids. Her response is, "Our enjoyment of any activity is enhanced when we know we're good at it" (p. 94). Teachers who love teaching love students, but they are seldom naive about the potential dastardliness of their cherubs.

The second author who has influenced me most is William Glasser (1990), who writes about reality therapy. Glasser writes with common sense that actions have consequences. As much as possible, the teacher tries to match consequences with behavior. Sometimes there are natural consequences. I remember the female student who struck a male student. Can one ever justify sufficient provocation for violence? That she broke her hand and that the male student was not physically hurt, and that they were still friends, was an indication to me that the natural consequences were sufficient. Most of the time, however, there are not necessarily natural consequences to irresponsible behavior. For example, what should the consequences be for tardiness? Having missed the class intros is rarely sufficient to change behavior.

I have a general policy not to punish myself for student misbehavior. Thus, I hate detention. It detains me. I also hate taking points off a student's grade. A grade should be an accurate indication of the quality of a student's academic work. And citizenship grades, when given, are rarely taken seriously by students. Thus, there needs to be a logical consequence to misbehavior. On a first or second tardy, I might use mild sanctioning. "Charles, you used to be my favorite student." But if the tardiness persists, you might ask the student to stay after class when the bell rings. That alerts other students to the fact

Figure 3.8. Some individuals are too kind, too sympathetic, too peace-loving ever to make very effective teachers.

that there is some consequence to being late. Virtually all students hate the idea of staying after class (and this is a better minute of your time to give up than one from your break or lunch or after school). If that doesn't work, the phone call home is a logical consequence. If that doesn't work, you have a problem that needs to be addressed more fully. The point here is the reality therapy of matching consequences with actions in a logical and reasonable way.

The greatest limitation to reality therapy is that it is one on one. I once saw a film in which the teacher demonstrated the techniques with a recalcitrant student right in front of the camera. To my huge delight as an experienced teacher, I was much more amused to watch the class, out of focus in the background, start falling apart and getting into fisticuffs. Reality therapy can work, if and when you can make sure the remainder of the class is responsibly occupied.

The better I got at handling discipline personally, the more I appreciated Alfred Alshuler's (1980) *School Discipline: A Socially*

Literate Solution. It is premised on the teacher being in the strong position and able to negotiate with students mutual solutions to discipline problems. This approach can be misperceived as coming from weakness because of the willingness to negotiate solutions with students. I think this method recognizes that there's more than one way to skin a cat. There's always more than one way to pass my class. A solution has to be okay with me, so I do not hesitate to probe solutions for students that might better meet their needs. Juan once told me he would rather flunk my class than give a speech (in my English class). He was quite serious. He did not earn an A in my class, which had a required speech component, but he was able to earn a respectable B and to entertain the other students on a camping trip, around the campfire, with stories that weren't official speeches. Alshuler (1980) is very good on negotiating for win-win outcomes.

Curiously, I "hate" the fourth book that influences me most—Canter and Canter's (1992) *Assertive Discipline*. Their techniques of specifying the required behavior and insisting that it be adhered to are sufficiently powerful that they can work even when what needs to be done is to change the curriculum. Their techniques tend to teach compliant behavior. My problem with compliant behavior is that you are no longer getting accurate feedback about your teaching. Nonetheless, I always try to emphasize that it is critical to keep your job to have the opportunity to improve your job. If you are failing at discipline, I recommend this book, but do not confuse that kind of discipline with teaching.

To sum up my suggestions about discipline, if you have interesting introductory, main, and concluding class activities and well-considered policies and procedures, you will have minimal discipline problems. But you will still have problems. Students must know their boundaries. Usually one student will take on the challenge of finding the limits. The key to your response is to divide and conquer. It is almost magical the difference in disciplining a student privately as compared to disciplining that student in front of the class.

How do you isolate that student?

1. Walk into the student's space without comment.
2. Whisper to the student.
3. Talk to the student just outside the classroom door. (Remind the student why you like him or her so much but why this particular behavior must change.)

4. Call the student's home.
5. Call for a parent conference.
6. Refer the student to the counselor.
7. Write a referral (this should be rare).

During any or all of these steps, commit yourself to believing and communicating to the student that you want to keep the student in your class, it is only a matter of an adjustment that needs to be made. That attitude alone will transform the climate of your classroom. Jenny Gray (1969) says that you will learn the most about teaching from your problem students. It might not be true, but believing it will give you an entirely different attitude about the problems you will have to solve.

Yea, though I walk through the valley of the shadow of death, I shall fear no evil.

Reading Levels and Discipline Problems

There is a very legitimate debate about the perils of watering down the curriculum. As an experienced teacher, my observation is that teachers tend to overestimate what they think students can already do when they first get them as students, but underestimate how much progress they can make in a term or year. Indeed, I am impressed that one of the best ideas in education right now is Hank Levins' idea about accelerating the curriculum for students who are behind in school. His idea is that teachers do students who are below grade level a disservice by having them work at an even slower pace. Such "consideration" results in these students falling even farther behind.

I tend to agree with those concerns. If your own students cannot read your assigned text, however, you are in trouble. And it is highly likely that many of your students will not be able to handle the texts that you have been assigned. So, what are you to do?

First, how can you tell ahead of time if texts are likely to be too difficult? A quick way of getting a good idea about how difficult your text is to do a Fog grade-level reading assessment of your text (see next section). It is a simple formula. It is only an estimation of grade level, but if you suspect your students are reading below grade level, and your Fog index comes out way above grade level, you undoubtedly have a problem.

The Fog Reading Level Index

1. Count 100 words of text. Divide by the number of sentences.
2. Count the number of words of three syllables or more. Do not count capitalized words, combinations of easy words (e.g., butterfly), or verbs with suffixes (e.g., creaking).
3. Take your answers to numbers 1 and 2 above and multiply by .4. This answer gives you an approximate grade level for the reading difficulty of that text. Try to make sure your sample of 100 words looks typical of your text, or take more than one sample.

Second, what do you do when the text is obviously too difficult for some, many, or all of your students? An answer, which has been called such things as "sheltered English," is to provide alternative ways of learning the core course concepts. The teacher can rewrite materials to an appropriate reading level. (I have done this, but be forewarned, it is very time-consuming.) You can lecture on key course concepts (and give clear accompanying notes or outlines that can be more easily read). You can see that the course material is covered through alternative media, especially visual and interactive media. You can try to find alternative texts written at the students' actual reading level. You can deliberately and specifically teach study skills that will help students raise their skill levels to that of the assigned texts.

There are no simple solutions. You do want to do everything possible to help students advance as far and as quickly as possible.

Third, stay aware of this issue! Every day! I became a reading specialist, and worked for a year as such at the high school level. I did this mainly because so many of my own failures as a first-year teacher were due to my students' inability to handle the assigned texts. Be aware, this is not only an academic problem. It is potentially the single biggest cause of discipline problems!

When I was hired as a high school reading specialist, my classroom was not yet ready. I had over a month to test all the students and to determine who, indeed, would be the best candidates for the reading program. I was not surprised that my classes ended up including virtually all the students who were either truancy and/or serious discipline problems. Rather than expose their reading "deficiencies" and embarrass themselves in front of their peers, these students chose alternative behaviors from a list that included being absent, acting out in disruptive ways, and causing actual physical confrontations in the class to avoid being embarrassed, behavior that did not seem related to the underlying academic issues, but was!

If you have five classes of 35 students, adjusting for the reading level for the range of student ability is overwhelming. What can be said more specifically than the general advice given previously? You do need to shelter your students so they can be protected while you work on their skills. You can offer as many alternative ways of learning your course objectives as possible. My four major strategies as a beginning teacher were (1) make sure I did not put a student into a potentially embarrassing situation like being asked to read aloud a passage that was too difficult; (2) make sure that 60-70% of the core material of the class was covered in as many ways as possible so that each student could have a realistic opportunity to pass the course; (3) never make the overall success of any lesson dependent on each and every student having successfully read the full text; and (4) periodically take class time to teach study skills that would help students do a better job with my subject area.

All the above is a major reason reading is a required course in many teacher preparation programs. Reading is crucial to success. I hope that you are much better prepared for this than I was. By all reports, I was a successful beginning teacher. What I remember clearly is my naked fear as I realized students could not handle my assigned texts and I had no idea what to do. As the anthropologist Jules Henry (1965) points out, fear of failure can be a powerful motivation. Although I do not think a teacher need increase a student's fear of failure—the culture has done that sufficiently already—I do recognize that my own early failure and fear of that failure made me a much better teacher as I explored every possible alternative that would help me overcome situations where students could not handle the texts provided.

In conclusion, there are no simple solutions, yet recognizing the tremendous significance and implication of material written at too difficult a level for students and working on solutions will avoid many, many discipline problems and make for more student learning and better teacher morale.

Miscellaneous Tips on Classroom Management

The hope is that this playbook will also be something of a reference guide. Maybe some karma, providence, or luck will lead you to back to a section that will help clarify a situation you are facing. I have generally organized this book around teaching and then management and discipline. In actuality, the overlap of areas in this book is as messy as teaching itself. Most of the other sections revolve around a fairly meaty topic like grading or homework. Following is a miscellany of the advice I have given in small pieces to other teachers over the years.

I have always found lists helpful. Following is a list of tips on discipline. They are the tips that I have had reason to pass on the most often to new teachers. Many are repeated elsewhere in these pages. In this form, they are quick reminders and have greater prospect of being immediately useful. They are most likely to connect when answering a particular need. The key is their timeliness. I think you will find that it is a good list to review periodically.

Tips on Things You Do as the Teacher

- Learn students' names the very first day. Do whatever necessary to learn them. This helps rapport and discipline immeasurably. I have started borrowing a video camera and asking all the students to tell me their names for the camera (and how I might best remember their names). I study the tape that first night. It takes several runs through the tape, but it works! The time is the best spent time of the term.
- Circulate. When you circulate through your class, you help keep students on task; help clarify and instruct students who need help; and have opportunity for friendly, personal interaction with others. And you can give special help to those behind and slow down those ahead so the class finishes about the same time.
- If materials are required for class, meet students at the door to remind them prior to the start of class.
- Take roll by identifying who is absent. Count those present and those marked absent and compare that total to the number registered in your class to verify the accuracy of your attendance count. This way, you catch anyone who answered "here" for a friend. Because most students are usually there, it is a lot quicker as an attendance-taking technique and you avoid spending time in an activity that is usually accompanied by minor discipline problems.
- A further hint about negative attendance taking: The students absent today are often the ones absent yesterday. If you ask the

Figure 3.9. Cultivate the misconception that you have eyes in the back of your head.

students, "Who is absent?" it helps make them aware and a little more concerned about each other.

- School bulletins are an important source of school communication, and, like Pavlov's bell, tend to make the listeners salivate and bark. Tell students briefly at the beginning of the term that you agree the bulletin is exceedingly important, and, with their cooperation, you can read it in 30 seconds. Then from each bulletin read the topics (e.g., Spanish club meets Thursday) and the occasional announcement everyone should hear, and then post the bulletin so anyone who needs more specific information will know to read it after class.
- Scan the class at unpredictable times, especially during tests. A favorite trick of mine is to identify someone doing something they shouldn't, like chewing gum, and then while my back is turned, ask them to throw it away. Cultivate the misconception that you have eyes in back of your head.

- If you are going to make students be seated at the end-of-class bell, make them go back to their seats before the bell rings to dismiss them, not after the bell has already rung. If the bell has already rung, not only might you look foolish when you are unable to control their exit, you might also be trampled to death.
- Don't leave your keys out—EVER!
- If your class is getting unruly or a little out of hand, give students a quiet seat assignment and call them one by one to come sit at your desk while you show them, in the record book, their string of grades for the term. This puts the troublesome students on notice; makes them a little wary; sobers them a bit; and helps get them back on task. You, in the meantime, can enjoy their discomfort while being very encouraging about how you know they are smart and can still do okay in your class. It is amazing how mesmerized some students become by a grade book.
- If you have to grab a student, grab him or her by the arm just below the armpit. Hair, necks, private parts can get you in trouble, but there's no real damage you can do the student by the arm just below the armpit.

Tips on Policies and Procedures

- Put assignments on the board. When students ask what they are supposed to do, just point at the board. It saves time and energy.
- Let students decide where they are going to sit. This doesn't allow you the convenience of a seating chart for learning names, or taking roll, or leaving it for the substitute teacher. It also tends to create more small problems like friends talking to each other. But in my opinion, that's better than friends yelling or passing notes to each other across class and allows students to sit away from each other when they are having problems with each other. Not only is letting them choose their own seats more democratic, it tends to minimize the likelihood of some bigger problems.
- Take a "deposit" of some personal possession of the student, such as a key ring, to hold until he or she returns the pen or pencil that he or she borrowed. Or let the student use pencils stubs and scratch paper that you provide rather than let the student disrupt your class. We all forget things sometimes, and it's just not worth the hassle to ruin your day on the inevitable.

- No permanent potty pass! Especially no tire irons or hub caps or other passes that will never be lost. If a kid has to go, be interrupted. It discourages unwarranted use of the request. If a kid needs to go often, the student has a bladder problem or you need to talk to him or her about how to make the course more enjoyable. Another idea is to have a nonpublicized three potty pass limit that you tell the student privately about after two trips. If the student needs to go a fourth time, okay it, but require an after-class or after-school discussion to stay honest with the intent of the policy.
- When you are passing out tests at the front of each row, count them out loud. It helps keep students from trying to latch onto an extra copy to take to a friend and helps perpetuate the image that you are well organized.
- Do not allow anyone into your desk. It compromises your authority. That's your private area.
- Ask students when they want tests. You can avoid having a test the day of the physics test or the day after the Super Bowl this way. You'll be seen as a decent human being. And you'll get better results and fewer complaints about the scores.
- Make your own rules and solicit student agreement. My one rule is: "no corn nuts." They smell terrible, especially on hot days. So of course students bring corn nuts every hot day. Then I yell, and then I am flexible and remind students of the larger issues of social contracts.

Tips on Attitudes to Cultivate

- Tolerate ambiguity. Don't try to make everything black and white. Emerson (1967) says a "foolish consistency is the hobgoblin of little minds." Leave yourself room for adjustments.
- Keep students guessing. Be a bit off the wall. Occasionally do something unexpected. It keeps them alert, less likely to mess with you, and more interested when you are not totally predictable.
- Appreciate differences. You've spent all your years finding out who you are and what you like and dislike. But now, as the teacher, you need to appreciate all the tastes, foods, human values, and cultural backgrounds of all your students. If you strive toward diversity in your instruction, you can give every

student a chance to succeed at something and to improve at something else.
- Divide and conquer. I like to divide my class up into four sections with a lane down the middle going from side to side of the classroom. I prefer my desk in the rear of one of the sections. If I absolutely have to talk to the entire class, I go to the middle, where the two lanes cross and I can be the center of attention. Otherwise, the four sections are convenient for small group or seat work. If I'm having trouble with a small group, I can isolate the group without distracting the other groups. Divide and conquer. If I'm having trouble with an individual student, I try to get him or her outside for a personal discussion. Divide and conquer.
- Laugh if it's funny. Don't be threatened.
- Be flexible. Don't paint yourself into a corner with arbitrary rules.

Notes

1. Reprinted with permission. From Emmer, E., Evertson, C., Clements, B., Sanford, J., & Worsham, M. (1981). *Organizing and Managing the Junior High Classroom*. Austin, TX: University of Texas.

2. These six rules have been adapted from a speech given by Mike Myers for the California Council of Teachers of Education.

3. Reprinted with permission. From Gose, M. D. (1984, October-November. "Classroom games and how to play them." *High School Journal*.

4

Thriving in Teaching

The Emergency Plan

The vanity of teaching often tempteth a man to forget he is a blockhead.
                              (George Saville, Marquis of Halifax)

I won't lie. No false modesty here. By all accounts, I had excellent success my first years of teaching. What I also want to emphasize is that you will never be prepared for the amount of failure you experience as a teacher. Ever. Hall of famer Ted Williams thinks hitting the baseball is the toughest athletic feat. Even the best hitters make outs 7 out of 10 times. Phillip Jackson (1968) reports that teachers have as many as 1,000 personal interchanges a day. You can bat .999 and still have a bad day (and sleepless night).

In fact, to thrive in teaching, you will find that you learn the most about teaching from your mistakes. I acutely remember how overwhelming it could all seem. I'd look for advice among other teachers, friends, journals, books, state frameworks, and district guidelines, and then pretty soon I'd start having something akin to anxiety attacks. It was overwhelming what I felt like I was supposed to know to teach.

I had to find something I could fall back on.

I needed a safety net.

To use a baseball image again, I needed something like the best advice on hitting: See the ball, hit the ball.

In this sense, even a survival guide would take too long to reread. I needed something equivalent to a cheat sheet, something very useful,

Figure 4.1. You must be able to withdraw to your basic game plan.

practical, close at hand. The emergency card is my answer to that need. If you are panicking, refer to this sheet. When you are feeling more confident, the remainder of this book is an expansion of these themes, with a tight focus on classroom realities. After you have created your own game plan, you will feel much more comfortable, even appreciative, of all those state reports and frameworks, syllabi, courses of study, teacher colleagues, journals, newspapers, and books that you can pick through judiciously to enrich your own teaching and to keep you interested in growing each year.

But the moment you start feeling overwhelmed, you must be able to withdraw to your basic game plan. I am confident that you can adapt my game plan and make it your own.

The Emergency Card

The Curriculum

Philosophy: Appreciate differences; diversify instruction

Lesson Plans: A, B, Cs (samples in Resources)

- A. An opening activity that settles class down while you take roll
- B. The major activity for the day
- C. An intrinsically interesting activity if your lesson comes up short

Discipline

- Realize and accept you can have great influence on your class, but you will never truly control it.
- If you are having general discipline problems, fix your curriculum.
- For conspicuous discipline problems, divide and conquer. ("See me after class." "Stand outside the classroom door and we will talk as soon as I can be there." Call the student's home.)
- Perambulate through your classroom! Your feet, not your voice, should be tired at the end of the day.

Other

- Be early and pick up your mail first thing so it is known you are there.
- Be especially nice to the principal's secretary and the school custodians.
- If you are feeling vulnerable, avoid the teacher's lounge.
- "Different not deficit!" You spent your life before teaching developing personal tastes and preferences. Forget that now. Make yourself learn to appreciate the varied strategies (and tastes and opinions) your students have developed trying to cope with life.

Finally

First and foremost, students, administrators, faculty, and staff go to school to live out each day. Make it a good day.

Thriving as a Teacher

. . . and we would all recognize for an instant the foolishness and absurdity of our ways through the world and feel the impact of the great, occasionally and accidental joy which would be our only reward along those paths.
(Herndon, 1971, p. 192)

Eventually, you should find that teaching is a great profession because you can never really master it. The growth possibilities are limitless. A teacher can add to his or her repertoire of skills, add to the playbook, add to the winning game plan, forever. Even if you have perfected all known teaching strategies and invented some new ones, there's always more to learn about each classroom member and how to match teaching with students.

This book emphasizes that a teacher is never prepared for the amount of failure experienced in a day. Nonetheless, teaching is potentially a richly rewarding profession. Every article, book, colleague, and student has the potential of providing a new insight that can lead to improved teaching. When the scope of this potential becomes too daunting, you can resort to the basics suggested by the emergency plan. There is a natural ebb and flow between trying out adventuresome new ideas and returning to the basics of your game plan. Without the ebb and flow, you would stagnate. Thus, in creating your own winning game plan, you should provide yourself with both a basic approach and room to grow to advance your repertoire of skills, ploys, and plans. You will get better and better at knowing when to take risks and when to play it safe. In the meantime, your early enthusiasm, extra energy, freshness, and inventiveness will serve you well. Do not be surprised by some professional jealousy among other teachers. They envy and maybe miss that special rapport that develops between students and new teachers.

The key to ongoing success will depend on your honesty with yourself. Quite simply, to thrive in teaching, you must recognize and accept that there is no place to hide—from yourself or your students. Certainly, you cannot hide behind your authority or your subject matter and still learn to enjoy your weeks and years. The key is to learn from what doesn't work and to celebrate your successes and your progress.

I suppose I have a bit less daily frustration after 30 years of teaching. But the difference is not as large as a beginning teacher might think. If it was easy, anybody could do it. The expectations rise. Just this past semester I had a college class of very bright students, some of whom I already knew well, yet the class was one of the biggest challenges of my career. Despite my 30 years of experience, the class required entirely new approaches, fresh solutions. Some frustration is an inevitable part of the motivation to improve the game plan.

That's largely why teaching stays interesting over decades. As fast as we are told that knowledge changes, most teachers can easily adapt

Figure 4.2. The key to ongoing success will depend on your honesty with yourself.

to those changes. It is the variation among students and personalities of classes that proves to be most challenging, and the most rewarding.

I laugh at reports that teachers found their teacher preparation programs inadequate. That's comparable to asking anyone if they make enough money. A running theme in these pages has been that you are never sufficiently prepared for the amount of failure you experience as a teacher. It is a primary condition of teaching: You are a flawed human being, working with unformed adolescents. The source of failure is also the source of delight, however. If you can accept learning from your failures, the learning becomes a pleasure. If you learn to love learning about your students as much as you love learning about your subject, each day has the potential to be a success.

It takes a while, but those early failures take on special meaning (after you heal). I can recall in a heartbeat, and tell with relish, the time I became so overly frustrated with my audiovisual equipment that a tiny swear word slipped from my mouth, or the time I was reading aloud to the class and too belatedly recognized an unfortunate euphemism for the male penis, or the time a student and I completely lost patience with each other, or letting Stan go early each day to the chess club so he wouldn't drive the entire class crazy.

I also remember getting a 16-year-old stutterer to the district speech therapist and seeing him quit stuttering before the term was out. I remember individual students who read their first book. I remember recognizing the voice of a favorite student 25 years later while crossing a street in an entirely different part of the state. For all the failures in teaching, the good memories make a deeper cache.

I have never been able to predict the good or bad days. Certainly there are days when one feels that a doctor, therapist, minister, and best friend are not possibly enough aide and counsel. Other days, you know that you might still teach even if you win the lottery. That is as true for me today as it was 30 years ago. I may have more influence over a class now, but a teacher never truly controls a class. In fact, it is probably somewhere in that seam between influence and lack of control that we find those moments James Herndon (1971) recognizes as the unexpected joys that are our rewards along the way.

Are these final words meant to be encouraging? Yes and no. Quite frankly, as I have suggested before, if you are unable or unwilling to take responsibility for your classroom, or if you are not student oriented, I cannot imagine that you will ever thrive in teaching. If you are willing to assume the leadership role as teacher, and if you are oriented toward your students, you probably won't find my encouragement all that necessary. If you are hooked on teaching, you don't likely need a lot of encouragement beyond that of your own relationship with students. If you are hooked on teaching, it is not likely you will be able to stay away from the profession.

It is probably time to admit that I quit teaching twice. The first time was related to feeling that I could not accomplish enough as a teacher. Having then tried social work for a short period of time, I had a renewed respect for what was possible for a teacher.

The second time I stopped teaching, I went back to work on an advanced degree. I had hardly started that course work when I found myself substitute teaching on Fridays. This choice was not entirely related to the day's wage as a substitute teacher. Personally, I have found it impossible to stay away from teaching, yet that has always gone hand in hand with days where I'd like to quit. Despite what you might otherwise think, most good teachers feel that strong ambivalence between loving and hating the job. I suspect that that ambivalence is related to our talent at learning from failure while hating it. Frustration can be a great motivator toward success. Success is always short-lived. Each day is a new challenge.

This book should be helpful in creating a game plan that makes sense for you. As you match your strengths with your students' interests, the game plan will lead quickly to early levels of success. Certainly, if you are able to find meaningful activities, isolate your discipline problems, and match your students' energy with a healthy sense of gamesmanship, you will be off to a good start. And you will have freed up enough time and energy to learn what you need to learn and to enjoy your classroom and your students. You will have time to hear or tell a joke, to observe the human condition, to offer an encouraging word, to frown dramatically when you are laughing inside, to marvel that you stand in that line of women and men fortunate enough to be called "teacher."

Resource A: Almost Instant Lesson Plans for Most Subjects

~ The Almost Instant Lesson Plan: English

I. Relation to Basic Academic Subject

   Reading and Literature
   ____ Read critically
   ____ Read analytically
   ____ Read with understanding a range of literature
   ____ Enhances interest and inquiry
   ____ Involves an imaginative response

   Writing
   ____ Recognize writing as a process
   ____ Write to discover and clarify
   ____ Write for different purposes
   ____ Develop skill and assurance

   Speaking and Listening
   ____ Engage in discussion as speaker and listener
   ____ Contribute succinctly
   ____ Present an opinion persuasively
   ____ Recognize intent of speaker
   ____ Recognize and take notes on important points
   ____ Recognize inconsistent logic

   Language
   ____ Recognize grammatical systems and patterns of usage
   ____ Language is constantly changing
   ____ English is influenced by other systems
   ____ Language is situational
   ____ Language has many dialects
   ____ Language is contextual

II. Primary Goal/Objective in a Sentence: The student will _____
   (behavioral verb)

   _____ .
   (content/subject)

	Probable Time Frame Minutes

III. Identify Activity

    A activity _____ _____

    B activity _____ _____

    C activity _____ _____

IV. Motivation: Why Will Students Do This?

    ____ It will be on the test   ____ It will connect with their lives

    ____ It is intrinsically interesting   ____ It has imagination/surprise

    ____ It is important to their future   ____ I'll force or bribe them

∾ The Almost Instant Lesson Plan: Art

I. Relation to Basic Academic Subject
   ____ Understand and appreciate the unique qualities of different media
   ____ Appreciate how different cultures use art
   ____ Appreciate different artistic styles from history and different cultures
   ____ Knowledge of the social and intellectual influences
   ____ Develop the skills, media, tools, and processes for self-expression
   ____ Identify and describe various art forms from different historical periods
   ____ Analyze the structure of a work of art
   ____ Evaluate a work of art
   ____ Express oneself in drawing, painting, photography, weaving, ceramics, sculpture

II. Primary Goal/Objective in a Sentence: The student will _____
   (behavioral verb)

   _____ .
   (content/subject)

III. Identify Activity   Probable Time
                                                        Frame Minutes

   A activity _____   _____

   B activity _____   _____

   C activity _____   _____

IV. Motivation: Why Will Students Do This?
   ____ It will be on the test   ____ It will connect with their lives
   ____ It is intrinsically interesting   ____ It has imagination/surprise
   ____ It is important to their future   ____ I'll force or bribe them

The Almost Instant Lesson Plan: Drama

I. Relation to Basic Academic Subject
   ___ Understand and appreciate the unique qualities of theater arts
   ___ Appreciate how different cultures use drama
   ___ Appreciate different artistic styles from history and different cultures
   ___ Knowledge of the social and intellectual influences
   ___ Identify and describe different kind of plays from different periods
   ___ Analyze structure, plot, characterization, language of a play
   ___ Express oneself by acting or otherwise participating in a dramatic art

II. Primary Goal/Objective in a Sentence: The student will _____
   (behavioral verb)

   _____.
   (content/subject)

III. Identify Activity   Probable Time
                                                          Frame Minutes
   A activity _____   _____
   B activity _____   _____
   C activity _____   _____

IV. Motivation: Why Will Students Do This?
   ___ It will be on the test   ___ It will connect with their lives
   ___ It is intrinsically interesting   ___ It has imagination/surprise
   ___ It is important to their future   ___ I'll force or bribe them

The Almost Instant Lesson Plan: Music

I. Relation to Basic Academic Subject

   ____ Understand and appreciate the unique qualities of music

   ____ Appreciate how different cultures use music

   ____ Appreciate different artistic styles from history and different cultures

   ____ Knowledge of the social and intellectual influences

   ____ Identify and describe various musical forms

   ____ Listen perceptively, distinguishing elements such as pitch, timbre, rhythm, dynamics

   ____ Read music

   ____ Evaluate a music work or performance

   ____ Express oneself by playing an instrument, singing, composing

II. Primary Goal/Objective in a Sentence: The student will _____
   (behavioral verb)

   _____ .
   (content/subject)

III. Identify Activity   Probable Time Frame Minutes

   A activity _____ _____

   B activity _____ _____

   C activity _____ _____

IV. Motivation: Why Will Students Do This?

   ____ It will be on the test   ____ It will connect with their lives

   ____ It is intrinsically interesting   ____ It has imagination/surprise

   ____ It is important to their future ____ I'll force or bribe them

The Almost Instant Lesson Plan: Dance

I. Relation to Basic Academic Subject

    ____ Understand and appreciate the unique qualities of dance

    ____ Appreciate how different cultures use dance

    ____ Appreciate different artistic styles from history and different cultures

    ____ Knowledge of the social and intellectual influences

    ____ Identify and describe dances of various cultures and historical periods

    ____ Analyze various techniques, styles, and choreographic forms

    ____ Evaluate a dance performance

    ____ Express oneself through dancing or choreography

II. Primary Goal/Objective in a Sentence: The student will _____

    (behavioral verb)

_____.

(content/subject)

                                                                                    Probable Time

III. Identify Activity   Frame Minutes

    A activity _____ _____

    B activity _____ _____

    C activity _____ _____

IV. Motivation: Why Will Students Do This?

    ____ It will be on the test   ____ It will connect with their lives

    ____ It is intrinsically interesting   ____ It has imagination/surprise

    ____ It is important to their future   ____ I'll force or bribe them

The Almost Instant Lesson Plan: Mathematics

I. Relation to Basic Academic Subject

   Basic
   ____ Apply mathematical techniques to solution of problems
   ____ Familiarity with language, notation, deduction
   ____ Express quantitative ideas with precision
   ____ Use computers and calculators
   ____ Familiarity with the basic concepts of statistics
   ____ Knowledge of algebra, geometry, functions

   Computing
   ____ Familiarity with computer programming and programs
   ____ Use of estimation to evaluate calculator and computer results
   ____ Familiarity with methods used to solve mathematical problems

   Statistics
   ____ Gather and interpret data and represent them graphically
   ____ Summarize data using such concepts as average, median, mode
   ____ Familiarity with techniques of statistical reasoning

   Algebra
   ____ Solve equations and inequalities
   ____ Develop skill in operations with real numbers
   ____ Simplify algebraic expressions, including simple rational and radical expressions
   ____ Work with permutations, combinations, simple counting problems, binomial theorem

   Geometry
   ____ Knowledge of two- and three-dimensional figures and their properties
   ____ Think of two-/three-dimensional figures in terms of symmetry, congruence, similarity
   ____ Use Pythagorean theorem and special right triangle relationships
   ____ Draw geometrical figures and use geometry to solve problems

   Functions
   ____ Knowledge of relations, functions, and inverses
   ____ Graph linear and quadratic functions and use them in problem solving

II. Primary Goal/Objective in a Sentence: The student will _____
                                                           (behavioral verb)

_____
                          (content/subject)

                                                    Probable Time
III. Identify Activity   Frame Minutes

    A activity _____   _____

    B activity _____   _____

    C activity _____   _____

IV. Motivation: Why Will Students Do This?

    ____ It will be on the test   ____ It will connect with their lives

    ____ It is intrinsically interesting   ____ It has imagination/surprise

    ____ It is important to their future   ____ I'll force or bribe them

The Almost Instant Lesson Plan: Science

I. Relationship to Basic Academic Subject

   ____ Distinguish between scientific evidence and personal opinion by inquiry

   ____ Recognize the role of observation and experimentation

   ____ Ask appropriate scientific questions

   ____ Recognize what is involved in experimental approaches to solutions of questions

   ____ Gather scientific information through laboratory, field, and library work

   ____ Organize and communicate results obtained through observation and experimentation

II. Primary Goal/Objective in a Sentence: The student will _____
   (behavioral verb)

   _____
   (content/subject)

III. Identify Activity   Probable Time
                                                          Frame Minutes

   A activity _____   _____

   B activity _____   _____

   C activity _____   _____

IV. Motivation: Why Will Students Do This?

   ____ It will be on the test   ____ It will connect with their lives

   ____ It is intrinsically interesting   ____ It has imagination/surprise

   ____ It is important to their future   ____ I'll force or bribe them

The Almost Instant Lesson Plan: History

I. Relation to the Basic Academic Subject

    ____ Basic factual knowledge of major political and economic institutions

    ____ Basic factual knowledge of social and cultural history

    ____ Knowledge of the content and concepts of the social sciences

    ____ Grasp of major trends in the contemporary world (e.g., nationalism, urbanization)

    ____ Familiarity with written, commercial, and visual forms of data

    ____ Understanding of the relationship of the present and past

    ____ Understanding of the problems of change over time

    ____ Recognize issues of cause and effect

    ____ Identify major historical turning points

    ____ Develop historical interpretations

II. Primary Goal/Objective in a Sentence: The student will _____

                                                                               (behavioral verb)

_____

                                   (content/subject)

                                                                        Probable Time

III. Identify Activity   Frame Minutes

    A activity _____   _____

    B activity _____   _____

    C activity _____   _____

IV. Motivation: Why Will Students Do This?

    ____ It will be on the test   ____ It will connect with their lives

    ____ It is intrinsically interesting   ____ It has imagination/surprise

    ____ It is important to their future   ____ I'll force or bribe them

~ The Almost Instant Lesson Plan: U.S. History

I. Relation to the Basic Academic Subject

　　____ Basic factual knowledge of major political and economic institutions

　　____ Basic factual knowledge of social and cultural history

　　____ Knowledge of the content and concepts of the social sciences

　　____ Grasp of major trends in the contemporary world (e.g., nationalism, urbanization)

　　____ Familiarity with written, commercial, and visual forms of data

　　____ Understanding of the relationship of the present and past

　　____ Understanding of the problems of change over time

　　____ Recognize issues of cause and effect

　　____ Identify major historical turning points

　　____ Develop historical interpretations

　　____ Knowledge of chronology and the effect of events and historical changes

　　____ Knowledge of the interaction among different peoples and cultures

　　____ Knowledge of events and historical trends in the United States and the world

II. Primary Goal/Objective in a Sentence: The student will _____
　　　　　　　　　　　　　　　　　　　　　　　　　　　　　　　　　(behavioral verb)

_____
　　　　　　　　　　　　　(content/subject)

III. Identify Activity　　　　　　　　　　　　　　　　Probable Time Frame Minutes

　　A activity _____　　_____

　　B activity _____　　_____

　　C activity _____　　_____

IV. Motivation: Why Will Students Do This?

　　____ It will be on the test　　　　　　　____ It will connect with their lives

　　____ It is intrinsically interesting　　　____ It has imagination/surprise

　　____ It is important to their future　　 ____ I'll force or bribe them

The Almost Instant Lesson Plan: World Geography and Cultures

I. Relation to the Basic Academic Subject

   ____ Basic factual knowledge of major political and economic institutions

   ____ Basic factual knowledge of social and cultural history

   ____ Knowledge of the content and concepts of the social sciences

   ____ Grasp of major trends in the contemporary world (e.g., nationalism, urbanization)

   ____ Familiarity with written, commercial, and visual forms of data

   ____ Knowledge of basic features of major societies and cultures

   ____ Understanding of the international context

   ____ Knowledge of similarities and major differences among the world's people

   ____ Knowledge of major events and movements in world history

II. Primary Goal/Objective in a Sentence: The student will _____
   (behavioral verb)

   _____
   (content/subject)

III. Identify Activity   Probable Time Frame Minutes

   A activity _____   _____

   B activity _____   _____

   C activity _____   _____

IV. Motivation: Why Will Students Do This?

   ____ It will be on the test   ____ It will connect with their lives

   ____ It is intrinsically interesting   ____ It has imagination/surprise

   ____ It is important to their future   ____ I'll force or bribe them

The Almost Instant Lesson Plan: Social Science

I. Relation to the Basic Academic Subject

   ____ Basic factual knowledge of major political and economic institutions

   ____ Basic factual knowledge of social and cultural history

   ____ Knowledge of the content and concepts of the social sciences

   ____ Grasp of major trends in the contemporary world (e.g., nationalism, urbanization)

   ____ Familiarity with written, commercial, and visual forms of data

   ____ Knowledge of basic information developed in the social sciences

   ____ Knowledge of basic methods of the social sciences

   ____ Ability to approach a social topic by means of the social sciences

   ____ Knowledge of economics, political science, psychology, sociology, anthropology

II. Primary Goal/Objective in a Sentence: The student will _____

   (behavioral verb)

   _____

   (content/subject)

III. Identify Activity | Probable Time Frame Minutes

   A activity _____ _____

   B activity _____ _____

   C activity _____ _____

IV. Motivation: Why Will Students Do This?

   ____ It will be on the test   ____ It will connect with their lives

   ____ It is intrinsically interesting   ____ It has imagination/surprise

   ____ It is important to their future   ____ I'll force or bribe them

The Almost Instant Lesson Plan: Foreign Language

I. Relation to the Basic Academic Subject

____ Ability to ask and answer questions

____ Maintain a simple conversation

____ Pronounce the language well enough to be understood

____ Understand questions and statements

____ Read and understand the written language

____ Write a paragraph

____ Deal with everyday situations

____ Knowledge of culture, history, life patterns

II. Primary Goal/Objective in a Sentence: The student will _____
(behavioral verb)

_____
(content/subject)

III. Identify Activity   Probable Time Frame Minutes

    A activity _____ _____

    B activity _____ _____

    C activity _____ _____

IV. Motivation: Why Will Students Do This?

____ It will be on the test   ____ It will connect with their lives

____ It is intrinsically interesting   ____ It has imagination/surprise

____ It is important to their future   ____ I'll force or bribe them

Resource B: Sample A, B, and C Activities

In Chapter 2, I describe the ABCs of teaching. The idea is that a teacher needs an A activity to open class, to help students settle into the class, and to give the teacher time to take roll. The B activity is the major vehicle for the lesson of the day. The C activity, which may become necessary when the B activity ends (or dies) before the end of class, is meant to keep the students involved and interested right up to the bell.

The sample lesson activities contained herein are primarily ones that I have used as an English teacher, but they are meant to serve as wide a variety of classes as possible. The activities are also meant to require only a modest amount of preplanning so that they can be used in a pinch. They are also intended to be suggestive. A successful teacher is a resourceful teacher. From the moment you become a teacher, you should automatically be on the lookout for materials that you might use for your class: news clippings, e-mail jokes, video clips, games, puzzles, readings, stories, songs. Find out what other teachers collect and horde materials that have the likelihood of working with future students. You will find it a lifelong preoccupation, much like a hobby. If any one of the following samples helps you, you have more on hand than I had my first year of teaching.

Also, let me emphasize, especially for the A and C activities, that the best possible alternatives are often ones that you have just "discovered." When you find something that you can use that day or that week, it has the advantages of probably having been found intuitively, will be fresher, more timely, and not have the same problems of copyright law that apply to materials for which you would have had reasonable opportunity to secure copyright permissions.

Sample A Activities

I have included sample A activities to start the class while you are taking roll. The A activities should have some inherent interest, the prospect of connecting with the students in a meaningful way. The following introductory activities can be adapted and used across a wide range of subject matters, including (in translation) languages. I have divided the A activities into five sections, suggesting that you could use one of each type at the beginning of each day of the week.

English teachers should not be the only teachers teaching vocabulary.

- What are key words for your subject? Identify these words and have students do something with them at the beginning of the period. You could have them look up key words in their text, put them in their own glossary, use them in a sentence.
- Have a contest and have students try to create the longest word that makes sense for your subject matter.
- Have students identify as many pairs of words that go together for your subject as they can. For example "split infinitive" in English, "manifest destiny" in history, "reciprocal relation" in math, "aerobic exercise" in physical education, "juvenile delinquent" in social science, "enlightened eye" in art.
- Create a list of favorite words. Here is mine:

Juxtaposition	Antithetical
Paradox	Enigma
Anthropomorphic	Dialectic
Irony	Incongruity
Ratiocinate	Heuristic

- Have students make up an insult using special vocabulary or strings of alliterated words that pertain to your subject (e.g., "You are a feckless zebu." "You are an obsequious sycophant." "You are a pusillanimous, pussy-footing, pink, pacifist puke.").

Once a week, you might open class by having students think about, talk about, and/or write about a well-selected quotation. I have divided a sample list of quotations into classic quotations and quotations that pertain to the student's education. Although most of these quotations may seem oriented toward college-bound students, I have found the underlying points applicable to all students. By limiting the length of the quotation, I find that most any student can benefit from puzzling out the meaning and significance. In fact, the quotations are often even more pertinent to the student who is struggling. The quotation may provide an insight that makes a difference.

Classic Quotations

- (To be used to set up a discussion of integrity) "To thine own self be true." (Polonius to Laertes in Shakespeare's *Hamlet*)
- (To be used to set up doing something new) "Some men see things as they are and say why. I dream things that never were and say why not." (George Bernard Shaw—often quoted by Robert Kennedy)
- (To be used when the issue is exceptions) "A foolish consistency is the hobgoblin of little minds." (Emerson, 1967)
- (To be used to encourage each student's creativity) "Insist on yourself; never imitate." (Emerson, 1967)
- (To be used to encourage individuality) "Who so would be a man, must be a nonconformist." (Emerson, 1967)
- (To be used when you think students are getting too stodgy) "From here on out, it's wish I hadn't instead of wish I had." (Quincy Jones)
- (To be used to set up the issue of appearances vs. reality) "It's not what it looks like you're doing when you're doing what it looks like you're doing. Express yourself." (Charles Wright, Watts 103rd Street Rhythm Band)
- (To be used when there's too much blame going around) "We have met the enemy, and they is us." (Pogo)

- (To ponder what makes us human; contrasts well with passion) "Cogito ergo sum." (I think therefore I am.) (Descartes, 1951)
- (To encourage student reflection) "The unexamined life is not worth living." (Socrates)
- (When someone thinks someone else is out to get him or her) "Just because you are paranoid doesn't mean they're not out to get you." (Yossarian, in *Catch 22*, 1961)

Quotations That Pertain to the Student's Education

- (To be used when you think your students are overly resistant to working with abstract language) "The University of Chicago program stressed and rewarded abstract analysis and relativity of values and judgment rather than fixed standards. Teachers introduced a good deal of ambiguity and often departed from conventional standards of judgment. It was precisely those students whose cognitive style inclined them to concrete thinking, to an insistence on one 'correct' answer, who made up the bulk of the academic casualties at the end of the year." (Alex Inkeles, 1968, p. 62)
- (To be used if there has been any issue of fairness in how popular students are treated) "(The teacher) is not entitled to suppress the distinction between high and low achievers, just because not being able to be included among the high group would be too hard on little Johnny . . . but teachers also like and indeed 'respect' pupils on bases independent of achievement status." (Talcott Parsons, 1968, p. 79)
- (To remind students of the joys of going to school) ". . . and we would all recognize for an instant the foolishness and absurdity of our ways through the world and feel the impact of the great, occasional and accidental joy which would be our only reward along those paths." (Herndon, 1971, p. 192)
- (To discuss what values are being taught in the school's hidden curriculum) "But what does differ is the recognition that universities also present students with a way of life, a set of standards, a distribution of students coming from particular social classes, and levels of academic achievement that will have an important impact on students. . . . Many parents as well as students recognize such qualities and guide their children to places whose implicit curriculum is compatible with their values and with the

levels of social, economic, and academic achievements to which they aspire." (Elliot Eisner, 1985, pp. 95-96)
- (When you are being accused of being too democratic as a teacher) "When you turn over the responsibility of a child's education to the child, they will not turn out like you wanted. But they weren't going to anyway." (Gose, n.d.)
- (To understand the positive side of the peer group better) "The peer group may be regarded as a field for the exercise of independence from adult control . . . provide(s) the child a source of nonadult approval and acceptance . . . is a field for acquiring and displaying various types of 'prowess.' " (Talcott Parsons, 1968, p. 77)
- (To consider what nonacademic skills are also important) "Effective participation in a modern industrial and urban society requires certain levels of skill in the manipulation of language and other symbol systems, such as arithmetic and time; the ability to comprehend and complete forms; information as to when and where to go for what; skills in interpersonal relations which permit negotiation, insure protection of one's interests, and provide maintenance of stable and satisfying relations with intimates, peers, and authorities; motives to achieve, to master, to persevere; defenses to control and channel acceptably the impulses to aggression, to sexual expression, to extreme dependency; a cognitive style which permits thinking in concrete terms while still permitting reasonable handling of abstractions and general concepts; a mind which does not insist on excessively premature closure is tolerant of diversity, and has some components of flexibility; a cognitive style which facilitates reasonably regular, steady, and persistent effort, relieved by rest and relaxation but not requiring long periods of total withdrawal or depressive psychic slump; and a style of expressing affect which encourages stable and enduring relationships without excessive narcissistic dependence or explosive aggression in the face of petty frustration." (Alex Inkeles, 1968, pp. 65, 66)
- (To explain your wide variety of teaching strategies) "The thrust of the educational experience should be towards diversity, not homogeneity." (Ray C. Rist, 1971, p. 107)
- (To consider how school socialize students in the hidden curriculum) "Schools teach students to (1) act by themselves . . . (2) perform tasks actively and master the environment . . . (3) ac-

knowledge the rights of others to treat them as members of categories . . . (4) on the basis of a few discrete characteristics rather than on the full constellation of them that represent the whole person. (Dreeben, 1968, pp. 63, 64)

- (To explain to students why you use so much variety in your classroom activities and why you may be different from other teachers they have had) "When we look at school curricula with an eye toward the full range of intellectual processes that human beings can exercise, it quickly becomes apparent that only a slender range of these processes is emphasized." (Ray C. Rist)
- (To warn students about the ideas that may unintentionally lead to trouble) "It is a very short step from the empirical notion that truth is what is verifiable by experience to the expansive belief that experience itself is valuable. . . . From there it is but another short step to the notion that the richest life is one that includes the most varied kinds of experiences . . . (This) emphasis on new experience may lead to a lack of regard for the quality and effects of experience, to the feeling that a bad trip may be better than no trip at all." (Orr & Nichelson, 1970, p. 96)

More Ideas

Once a week, work on various approaches to questions.

- Have students write five possible questions for the next exam.
- Have students write 10 questions that will not be put on the exam that show their best insight into your text. (Questions 3-8 usually offer great insight into the quality of work the student is doing. The first two get them going, and 9 and 10 encourage them to think hard at least through the eighth question.)
- Play "20 Questions" with something in mind about your subject matter.
- Have students write answers to the who, what, when, where, why, and how questions.
- Do an exercise where questions can be responded to only with further questions.
- Have a student make any statement and see how many times in a row the same student can answer why over and over.

Once a week, start class by requiring some reading.

- Have students use the index and other features of your text to locate key information.
- Have a 5-minute timed reading test. Have students read for understanding. Multiply the average words per line times the number of lines read and divide by 5. Typically we speak about 225-250 words a minutes, but can read much faster than that. 400 words per minute is respectable for college work. (Watch for students with moving lips—it means they are reading out loud to themselves. Mention that this practice slows them down.)
- Have students read in their text in preparation for the B activity.
- Have students find something in the class set of newspapers.
- Have students read a handout.
- Have students do sustained silent reading in a book of their own choosing.
- Have students write notes to each other and then read them.
- Have students look up key words in the dictionary.

Be prepared to have a more enjoyable activity to liven the class. These samples may be helpful.

- On a sleepy day, sing and act out: The Grand Old Duke of York; he had 10,000 men. He marched them up a hill and then he marched them down again. And when you're up, you're up. And when you're down, you're down. And when you're only half-way up, you're neither up nor down. (three times)
- In 1 minute, list everything you could do with a rock, a chair, and a marble.
- In 4 minutes, list as many things or actions that are impossible to do.
- Unscramble these phrases:

    The trees another gets—shade plants the one generation.
    (One generation plants trees—another gets the shade.)

    The don't wear out words kind tongue.
    (Kind words don't wear out the tongue.)

    For the too little nothing man to whom enough is enough.
    (For the man whom enough is too little, nothing is enough.)

- Unscramble these words:

    TULCAFY—faculty
    RESION—senior
    BLUC—club
    SOWNG—gowns
    CANED—dance

- Unscramble this sentence: "Enverd si het ipacalt fo Colodaro" (Denver is the capital of Colorado)
- For 3 minutes, list the consequences if suddenly everyone became deaf.
- List 10 uses for a wheelbarrow.

    Place the words below in their correct order:

    Is the sun under nothing there new
    Do what for not you ask your country can

- Unscramble the following letters to make words:

    drows
    aefrugript
    telf
    drenu
    kas

- Write five consequences or results of what would happen if suddenly everyone became 2 feet taller.

Sample B Activities

I include sample B activities that can serve as the major activity for the class period. They are flexible and can be used in a number of ways across a number of subject areas.

- I like to use a "hearing" format, where each student is responsible to testify individually. Students can represent a literary character or historical person. Each represents his or her assigned "views," and a jury deliberates a conclusion. Trials can work well, too, in virtually any subject. My problem with trials is that they are only as good as the prosecuting and defense attorneys, and it is not always possible to find students who fulfill those two roles well. With a hearing, you can be the judge and/or congressional committee and keep things moving.

- The five-paragraph essay: If your students are not organizing their papers or essay questions very effectively, you might want to teach them the five-paragraph essay regardless of whether you are their English teacher. (See Figure R.1.)
- A new-old pattern for classroom interaction: The beauty of this idea is its simplicity. You can use it in kindergarten through graduate school. You can use it in any subject matter. You can use it with any number of students over two. In using the idea, you simultaneously help students get to know each other better while helping them practice what sociologist Robert Dreeben (1968) calls the necessary "formation of social relationships more transient, more time bounded than those characteristic of the family." The idea is undoubtedly an idea you are already familiar with. You just probably never thought of applying it to classroom practice (see Gose, 1986).

The idea is to use the round-robin tournament format from athletics in your class, but not for sports or competition. Instead of having a basketball tournament, or tennis championship, or checkers competition, you can pair students off to accomplish an educational task. You can have them discuss a series of issues, answer a number of subject matter questions, compare attitudes, identify favorites, and learn something about each other.

You can use the format to ensure that every student interacts personally with every other student in a positive, constructive way. In the round-robin tournament format, team 1, or in this case student 1, stays in the same place and the other students rotate counterclockwise. Thus, if you have only six students the tournament will look like this:

Assignment	A	B	C	D	E
	1—6	1—5	1—4	1—3	1—2
	2—5	6—4	5—3	4—2	3—6
	3—4	2—3	6—2	5—6	4—5

Within five "assignments," each student sees every other student exactly once. If you have an odd number of students, you can participate, making an even number. If each assignment takes 10 minutes, one rotation or cycle in this example would take 50 minutes. A + B + C + D + E (each of which is 10 minutes) = 50 minutes. If you have 50 students, who spend 1 minute on each assignment, the cycle will take 49 minutes.

I do not recommend using this format often. I use it as a change of pace. If I have been lecturing too much and I want to make sure every student has an opportunity to discuss some specific questions, I'll send them through a complete rotation. If I think the students are becoming cliquish, I'll find a reason to send the class through a complete rotation.

I value knowing who has the right answer as much as having the right answer. It's how I get my body, car, and toaster fixed. To review for a test, or even to take a test, I'll send students through the rotation, allowing them to "cheat" by asking help from the person they are paired with, one pairing at a time. Often it's not the person who "knows" the most who gets the highest score.

I am consistently amazed at how adept students are at beginning and ending a conversation, even if they only have a minute or two to talk to the other person. I am consistently amazed at how involved my otherwise shy students become when given the opportunity to talk with just one person at a time. I am consistently amazed at what a pick-up this activity can be during an otherwise slow period with a class.

I recommend you do not use this for one-on-one competition unless it is a nonthreatening one-on-one game. I strongly recommend you use your own imagination to decide what you want each group of students to do together in completing their assignment. I recommend each new pairing have a new assignment, task, or question to prevent boredom and comparisons. I also recommend using tasks, questions, and assignments both members of the pair will be able to talk about. With a group of 30 students in teacher education, I'll ask 29 different questions. Who was your favorite teacher and why? What's a way of getting a class quiet you've seen and liked? What rules should a class have? In less than 90 minutes, I can maximize students' opportunities to talk. (Hart, 1978, contends that we learn by talking.) And, in the remaining 30 minutes of my 2-hour class, I have students report some of their more remarkable "discoveries."

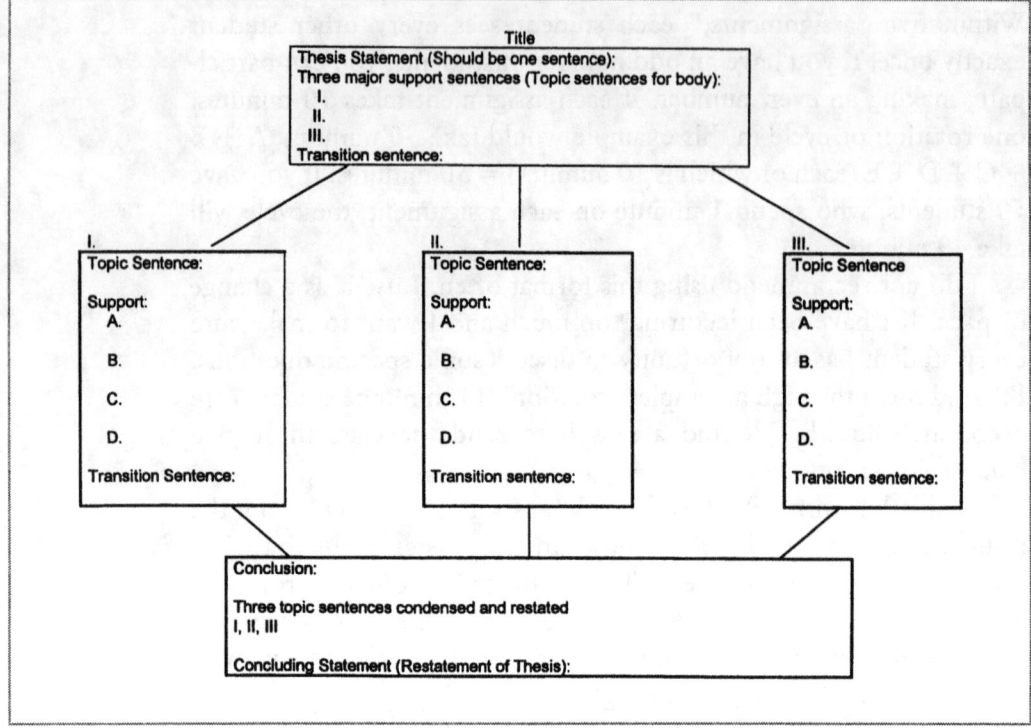

Figure R.1. Outline for the Five-Paragraph Essay.

Try it. I think you will like this new way of using an old idea.

- Tear a magazine or book into separate parts for oral reports on each section. This is a relatively inexpensive way to bring enrichment materials into the classroom. You need only one copy of the original. And students need work in summarizing material orally.
- Following is a list of 25 words college professors like to see on essays. Have your students work these terms into a paper or conversation about your subject.

I asked 15 professors who teach college freshman seminars to identify 10 words they like to see used by students in essays. I compiled this list of words and eliminated words that were too specialized (i.e., pertained to only one subject). I then asked the professors to rank the usefulness of each word. *Useful* was defined as meaning the word could be used (1) across subject matters; (2) in several essay situations; (3) to make a significant, intelligent point; (4) as a fresh (not overused) term. The words were scored on the basis of 0 for not useful; 1 for useful; 2 for very useful. I compiled the results and identified the 25 highest rated words.

Inclusive	Aesthetic	Resolute
Infer	Empathy/sympathy	Supersede
Imply	Plausible	Salient
Coherent	Tenuous	Substantiate
Sequential	Recapitulate	Accentuate
Augment	Autonomous	Pragmatic
Dichotomy	Expedient	Criteria/criterion
Effect/affect	Ambivalent	
Retrospective	Disseminate	

- Picture password: I mainly use this activity for the energy it creates. But I also use it to introduce the issue of intelligence. Stoddard once defined intelligence thus:

   Intelligence is the ability to undertake activities that are characterized by (1) difficulty, (2) complexity, (3) abstractness, (4) economy, (5) adaptiveness to a goal, (6) social value, (7) the emergence of originals, and to maintain such activities under conditions that demand concentration of energy and a resistance to emotional forces. (in Gage & Berliner, 1979, p. 74)

   This game evidences all those qualities.
   Students should be grouped in teams of three or four. One member of each team is given the same word to communicate to the other team members. The only clues that they can give their team, however, is those that they can draw. No letters or numbers are permissible. The first team to guess the word wins the point. Play to 10 or 15 points. Have a procedure for determining who really was first because near ties are frequent. The noise level also gets high, so check to see that your neighbors aren't giving tests.

- Haiku: Students can write haiku about any subject matter, and it may include some students who are ordinarily left out.

   Haiku has 17 syllables in 3 short lines:

   5
   7
   5

Haiku conveys a single image, mood, emotion, or thought. For example,

> Under a spring mist,
> Ice and water forgetting
> Their old difference.

Because Haiku is translated from the Japanese, it sometimes varies slightly from this pattern.

- Cinquains: I often teach Cinquains with haiku. Students who have problems with haiku can always do Cinquains. Again, you may include some students writing about your subject who had otherwise been struggling.

Cinquains are five lines of poetry written to the following formula:

Form	*Sample*
A noun	Gose
Two verbs	teaches, professes
Three adjectives	wise, resourceful, sagacious
A phrase or clause	a real modest guy
A synonym for the noun in line 1	Gose writer

- Stop, look, and write: This is the title of both a worthwhile paperback book and an approach to writing. Present one or several large pictures and have students write down what they see. Choose a picture that reflects your subject matter. The pictures tend to lend themselves to good writing.
- The form of social science research: If you have students do research, this is a good form for organizing the report of that research.

   1. Identify problem
   2. Review the literature
   3. Describe the instruments and the population
   4. Report the treatment
   5. Present and discuss the results
   6. Project possible implications

- The family interview: A very valuable exercise is to have students generate questions related to your subject and go home and formally interview family members.
- Athletic event: Stage a classroom athletic event and then have students draw, write, critique, paint, or whatever other activity would relate the event to your subject matter. For example, a Spanish class could describe the event in an essay written in Spanish.
- Newspaper: The newspaper will be a major source of information following graduation. Get a classroom set of newspapers and make an assignment appropriate to your subject matter.
- Guest speakers: Invite someone interesting to speak to your class. Don't make them speak the whole hour, though. If things lag, interview the person.
- A letter: Have students write themselves a letter and promise to mail it to them in a year. Ask them to relate at least part of it to your subject or school. You could also have them address a letter written in class to a famous person, a relative, someone in the school, a politician, and so on.
- Have students give impromptu speeches on videotape and play them back. You can help them become more articulate about your subject.
- Have students draw a map establishing relationships among your major course concepts.
- If each student will contribute about a dollar, you can have each member of the class write or draw something that you can then have photocopied and bound as a class project.
- Have the students respond to some aspect of your subject matter in terms of the five senses.
- Have students find your course themes in popular music or in movies and play the four or five best examples of connecting popular culture to your subject. (Do be careful to screen the language before you have these segments played in class.)

Sample C Activities

These activities are on the creative side. They tend to be on hold for emergencies. That emergency may be that your lessons have been a bit

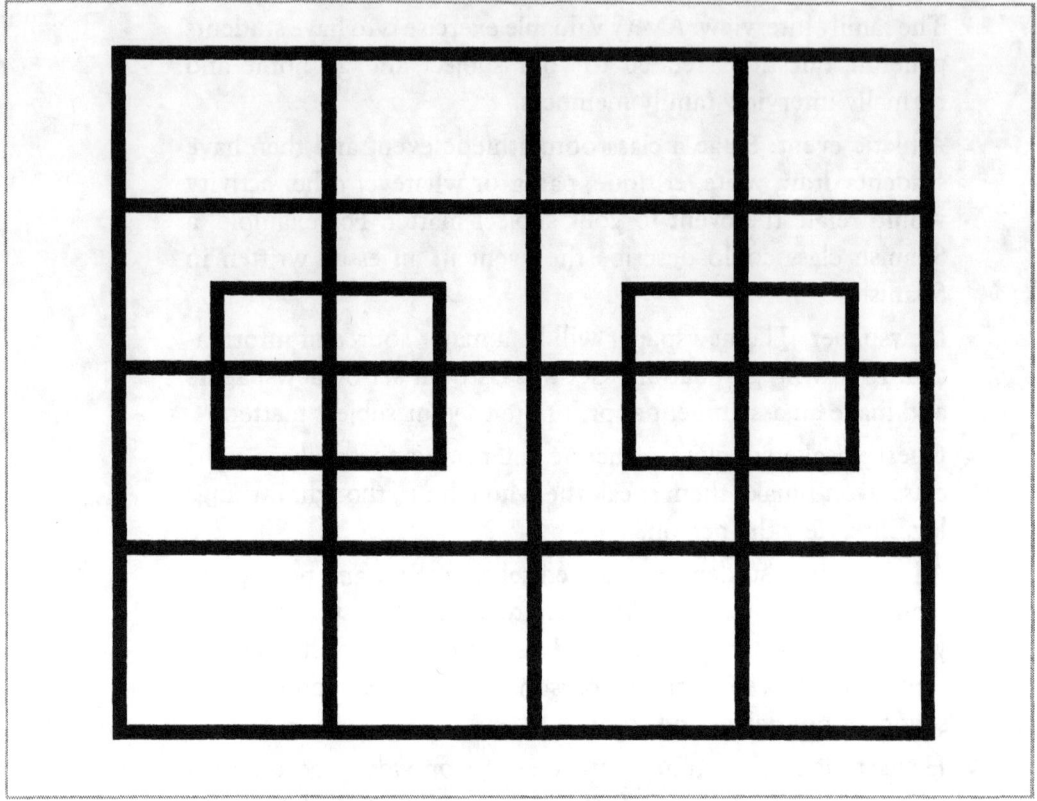

Figure R.2. How many squares are there?

boring lately and you need a change of pace. Do not hear from this that you should in any way neglect your course requirements.

These sample C activities have the prospect of holding your students' attention on days when your main lesson finishes early. These activities are mindful of the potential discipline problems that occur when a lesson comes up short, but they also promise to help students with flexible thinking.

- "How Many Squares Are There?" will keep most students occupied, and keep the others from interfering with their attempts to be the first one with the right answer (Figure R.2).
- I've often been able to salvage the last few minutes with examples of drawing a figure without lifting one's pencil (Figures R.3, R.4, R.5, R.6).
- The boxes that add up to 15 no matter which three you count in a row can take a while, but is reasonably doable (Figure R.7).

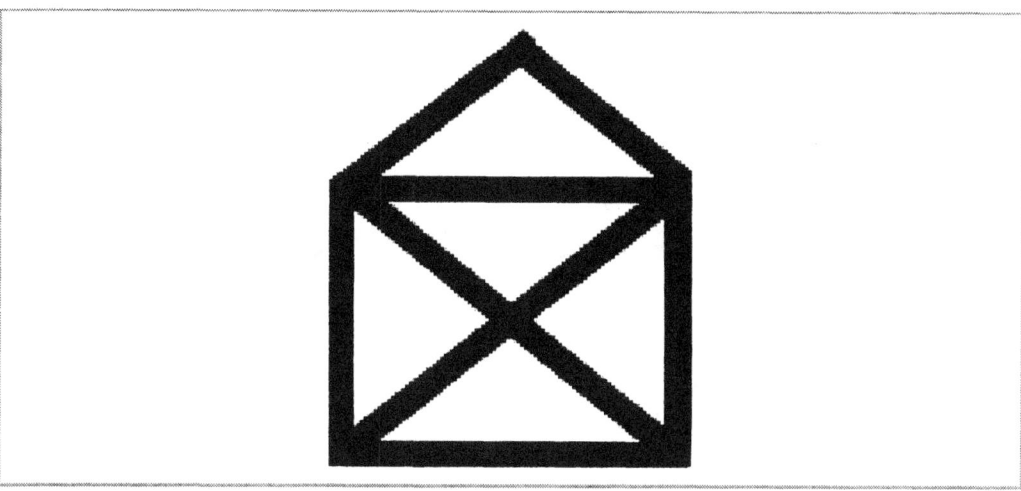

Figure R.3.

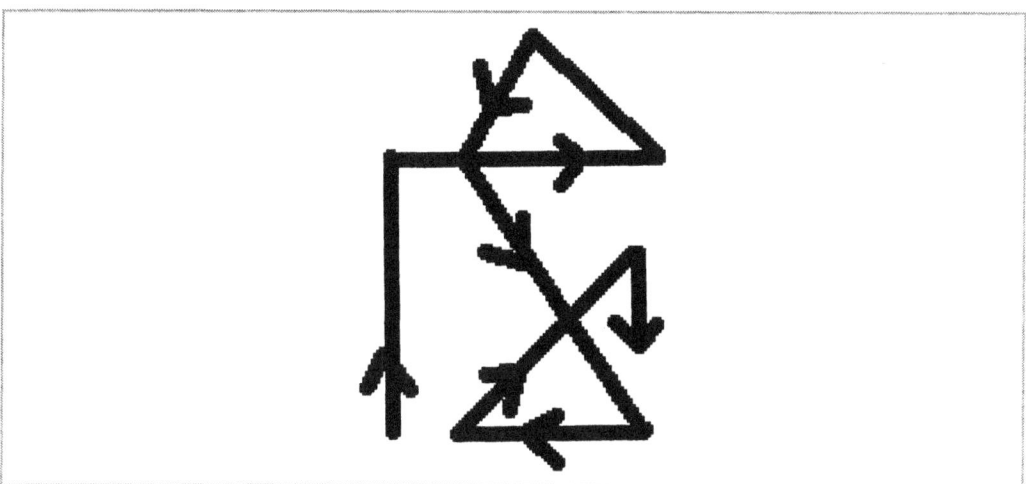

Figure R.4.

- I've used the nuns and whales story in a number of classroom settings. It is an excellent version of the old "20 Questions" and is purportedly based on a true story.

At Marine World one day, the dolphins wouldn't come up for their scheduled performance appearance. Before and after this one occasion, they never failed to appear. What happened?

Students can ask you any question and you must answer honestly, but with only a yes or no answer.

188 CREATING A WINNING GAME PLAN

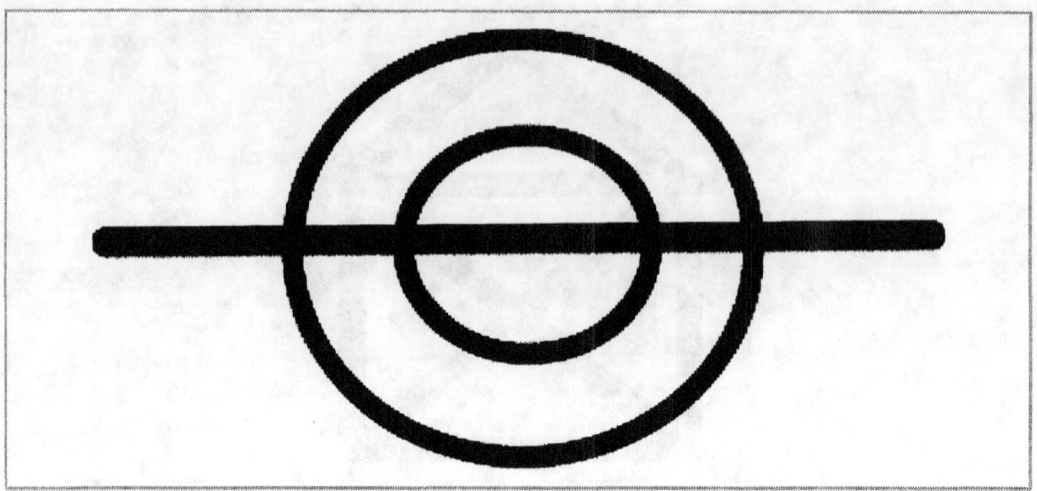

Figure R.5.

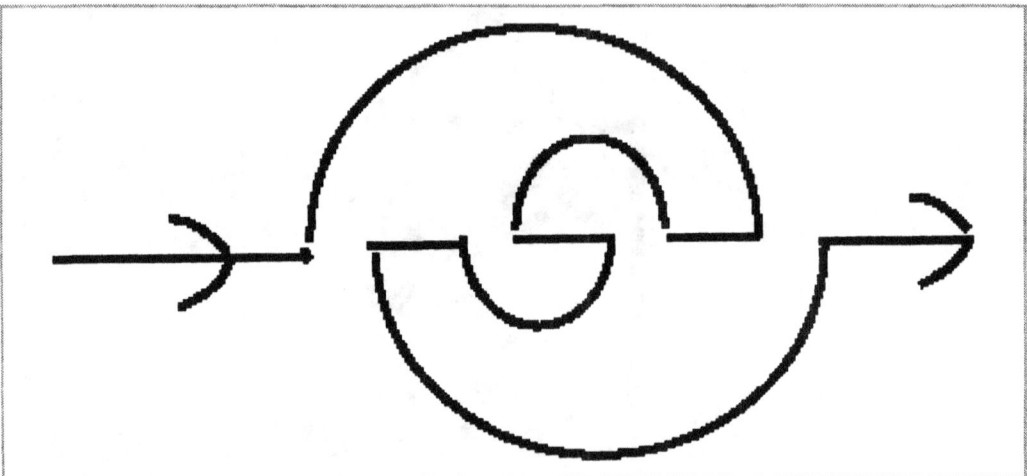

Figure R.6.

What happened was that the performance was attended by a large group of nuns in their habits. Apparently the black and white garb smacked of whaledom. The dolphins didn't come out.

- I have had grand success with the Wacky Wordies that sometimes appear in *Games* magazine. Have students make up their own. Here are five examples.

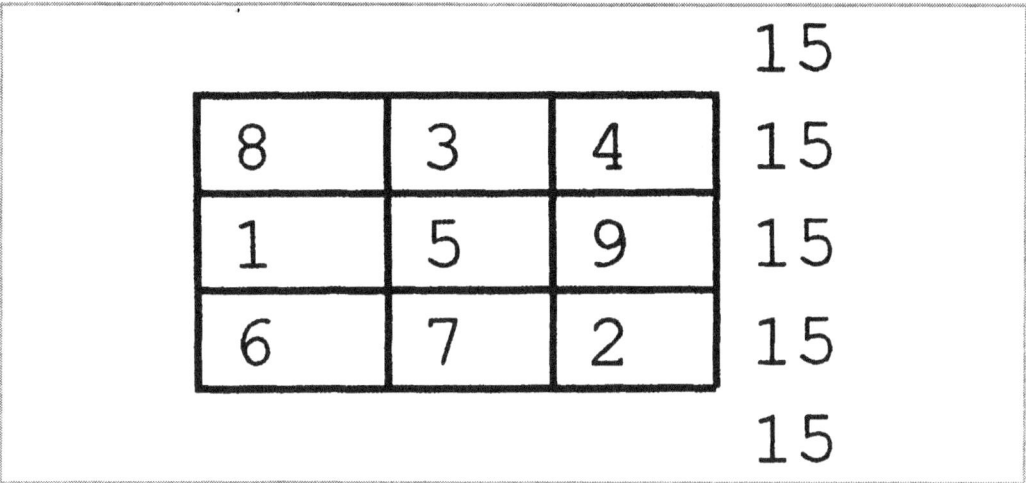

Figure R.7. Boxes that add up to 15, no matter which 3 you count in a row.

T
O
U
C
H
(touchdown)

LU   CKY
(lucky break)

bad bad
(too bad)

arrest
you're
(you're under arrest)

neckCLAMS
(small neck clams)

- "How Many Triangles Are There?" (Figure R.8) is comparable to Figure R.2 on squares.
- I get a lot of mileage asking students about the longest word in English. Here are three candidates. You can show off your spelling on the chalkboard.

    pneumonoultramicroscopicsilicovolcanoconiosis
    (black lung disease)

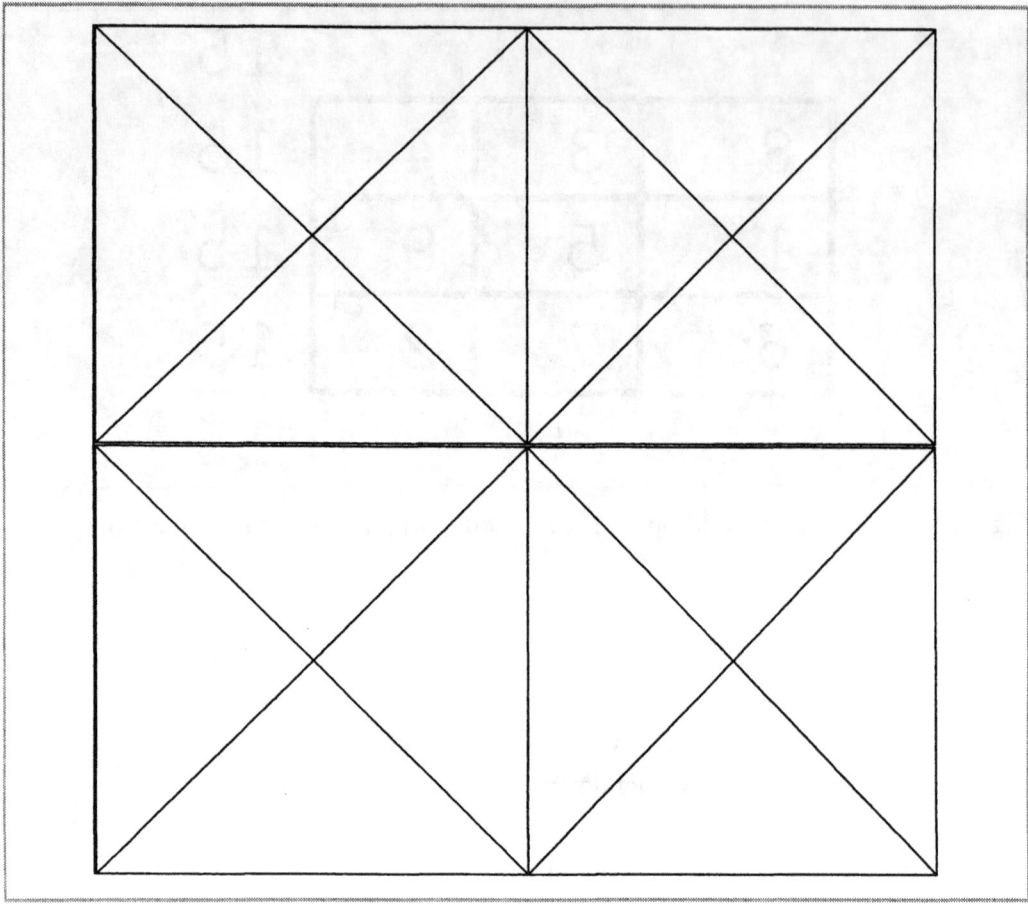

Figure R.8. How many triangles are there?

> antidisestablishmentarianism
> (against tearing down institutions)
>
> supercalifragilisticexpialidosius
> (wonderful, from Mary Poppins)

- I've also gotten a lot of end-of-class mileage by sputtering out the following:

> The stupid skunk sat on a stump; the skunk thunk the stump stunk, the stump thunk the skunk stunk. (alliteration)

> I have a cousin in Arkansas. His name is Esau. He has a saw that can outsaw any saw you ever saw. If you ever saw a saw that can outsaw Esau's saw, you saw more than I ever saw. (assonance)

- I am still amazed by how many students cannot answer this question:

    A young boy was in a car accident with his father and grandfather. Both the father and the grandfather were killed instantly. The little boy was rushed to the operating room. But the doctor said, "I can't operate on this boy. He's my son." Explain. Answer: The doctor is the boy's mother.

- This one always works well because, despite students' great interest in money, they pay very little attention to its details. "Who are Mary Withersen, Robert Rubin, Lloyd Bentsen, Nicholas Brady? You do not need to leave your seat to find this answer. Relax/meditate. Look within." (Answer: treasurer and secretaries of the treasury—identified on U.S. paper currency.) What do the Latin phrases mean on your money?

    e pluribus unum: out of many, one
    novus ordo seclorum: a new order of the ages

- Offer an A for the day to anyone who can answer all these general knowledge questions:

    Who wrote the autobiography of Samuel Johnson?
    What is the most commonly used word in the English language?
    Who is buried in Grant's tomb?
    The San Francisco Museum announced that it has discovered a coin dated 15 BC. Do you believe it? Why?

- If you have some amount of time left in the period, you can pose timely ethical issues that have appeared in the news. For example:

    A man and wife who were unable to bear children contracted with a second woman to bear them a child. For several thousand dollars, this second woman agreed to be artificially inseminated by the man and deliver the child after birth. The child was born with Down's syndrome. The man and woman would not accept the child nor pay the second woman the specified amount. The "mother" did not want the child, but she did want her money. The case went to court. Who should have the baby? The man and woman? The "mother"? The court? Should the man and woman pay the mother? Who should pay the court expenses?

Feel free to play devil's advocate to get at all the issues. As a matter of fact, in this case it was determined the "mother" was not pregnant via artificial insemination but by her husband. Thus, the issue is still unresolved, but may very well happen again.

- "A nickel if you can spell both seize and siege correctly (with confidence)."
- "Recite something (clean) that you know from heart. The words to a song are okay."
- Ask students to relate their best, tellable, embarrassing moment.
- If you have 30 students in your class, for some reason it seems 50/50 that two will have the same birthday. Ask and see.
- Ask if anyone will sing a song.
- Compare genetics. Can you flare your nostrils? Do you have ear lobes? Do you have hair on your knuckles? Can you wiggle your ears? Do you have a widow's peak? Is your second toe longer than your big toe? Can you touch your nose with your tongue? Do you have an Adam's apple? Can you touch your wrist with your fingers? Are you devilishly good looking?

Some may object that the C activities are not as academically oriented. They aren't. As Charles Dickens says, "The people must be amused." But these "games" help promote flexible and creative thinking, and often help with the rapport between teacher and student.

Good teachers are generally very resourceful teachers. It would be worth your while to undertake the following scavenger hunt.

Resource C: A Scavenger Hunt to Encourage Resourcefulness

Identify five videocassettes you could use in your class that are available at Blockbuster or some other local video rental agency.

Write the phone number to receive a class set of your local paper.

Identify 1 videotape; 2 audiocassettes; 5 books; 2 magazines; 2 books on tape that you could use in class from the county library.

Identify a source for used books and magazines (that cost $1.00 or less each).

Identify a publisher who has books you might like and write for their catalogue.

Identify a methods textbook in your subject matter area.

Identify a magazine in your subject area.

Identify a store that carries *Games* magazine.

Gather some of your own A, B, and C activities.

List five people you'd like to have as guest speakers or teachers in your class who might actually be able to do so.

~ Resource D: Homework Assignments

I wanted to add a few sample homework assignments. I also have some strong recommendations. First, always assign some sort of homework Monday through Thursday, but not the kind you have to collect daily. Second, never assign homework over the weekend. Do you hate youth that much? Third, try to minimize the busy work. It's not clear students need busy work, and you surely do not need more papers to grade. Use your tests to account for the reading as much as possible. Fourth, be very careful how you do handle homework. Some of your best students will not do it. Some of your "worst" students may be facing circumstances that mitigate against it. My suggestion is to let it help a grade without it being an absolute prerequisite for passing your class.

I highly encourage using homework to promote the cultivation of relationships and the start of lifelong learning.

- Have the students interview their parent or guardian about selected issues pertaining to your class.
- Have the students do a good deed, maybe unexpectedly wash the dishes or mow the lawn, but without saying why. Then have them report back. It makes for a good oral report or social study.
- Require students to get a library card.
- My favorite assignment: Have students write down 10 questions about what they are studying. Promise them they will not have to answer these questions. This will give you great insight into the level of work your students are doing.

- Have students watch a particular program on TV.
- Have students look for a particular news story in the newspaper, magazines, or TV.
- Have students prepare a demonstration and tell about some aspect of what you are studying. For example, I have always wanted students to try to find something from every country in the world.
- Have students go to an event and report back on its relationship to what you are studying.
- Have students find some sort of reference to your subject matter in a popular song.
- Have students use the phone and/or computer to locate information about your subject matter.

Resource E: Annotated Resources

∼ Friendly Books to Cheer Your Efforts

Ashton-Warner, S. (1963). *Teacher.* New York: Bantam. One of the classic books by a teacher about her experiences teaching elementary school in New Zealand.

Gray, Jenny. (1968). *Teaching without tears.* Palo Alto, CA: Fearon; and (1969). *The teacher's survival guide.* Belmont, CA: Pitman. Both these books are now out of print. I tried unsuccessfully to locate Ms. Gray. These books are still very relevant and were the greatest help of any outside resource to me in my first 2 years of teaching. I still highly recommend them if you can find copies.

Herndon, J. (1968). *The way it spozed to be.* New York: Simon & Schuster. This was Herndon's first book about his first year of teaching. Despite his struggles, when there was a riot at his school, it was his students who acted responsibly. Helping students take more responsibility for their lives is what I consider to be the underlying curriculum of all teaching.

Herndon, J. (1971). *How to survive in your native land.* New York: Bantam. I have read this book dozens of times. I have read this book more than any other. It captures what it means to be a teacher better than any other book I have ever read. It is especially rare in that it is a book written by a person who had a full career in public school teaching.

Herndon, J. (1985). *Notes from a schoolteacher.* New York: Simon & Schuster. This is the third and last of Herndon's books about his own teaching experiences. Herndon, because of his great sense of humor and irony, has often been compared to Kurt Vonnegut.

Inchausti, R. (1992). *Spitwad sutras.* Westport, CT: Greenwood. This book deserves much attention. This is a highly intelligent book, although again about first-year teaching, but in this instance set in a boys' parochial school, that gets at the ambition to teach the sublime.

Johnson, L. (1992). *My posse don't do homework.* New York: St. Martin's. This is the book that was the inspiration for the film *Dangerous Minds.* It has the advantage of being the latest book to depict the universal themes of good teaching in a recent setting.

Kane, P. R. (Ed.). (1991). *The first year of teaching.* New York: Walker. This offers excellent perspective on the first year of teaching.

Mathews, J. (1988). *Escalante.* New York: Holt. This is the book about the teacher depicted in the film *Stand and Deliver.* Mathews calls him the best teacher in America.

Tolstoy, L. (1967). *Tolstoy on education.* Chicago: University of Chicago Press. Reading about the teaching done by one of the world's greatest authors is inspiring!

Movies

Why Shoot the Teacher? (1977). A film about a teacher (Bud Cort) who goes to a rural, Canadian school during the Depression for his first year of teaching. This film captures what it feels like to be a teacher more than any other film I have ever seen. It is a small treasure.

My Bodyguard (1980). This film is primarily about students who happen to be in high school. The scene of the first day of class with Christopher Makepeace and Matt Dillon is the best-handled single scene of high school teaching I have seen. It is exceptional. Be sure to note two points. The teacher honors her own mistake in how she handles a potential discipline situation. She clearly recognizes the importance of the teacher's duty to protect her students.

To Sir With Love (1967). In some ways a dated film, but Poitier is great, and how he implements the divide and conquer rule is not to be missed.

Fast Times at Ridgemont High (1982). Not a very good film per se, but the Sean Penn "Spiccoli" character is inspired, and the classroom scenes with Mr. Hand are great!

The Breakfast Club (1985). Although this film may seem stereotypical to an experienced teacher, it is an illustration of the functions of the peer group, and the roles of the nerd, jock, malcontent, cheerleader, and brain continue to be real to high school students.

Mr. Holland's Opus (1995). This is one of the rare movies that depicts a teacher's career (instead of the usual first-year teaching saga). Although a bit over the top, it does get at the influence students can have on the teacher and the way the struggle enables.

Heathers (1989). Black comedy. See it as a parable, not a drama. This takes the worrisome aspects of high school peer groups and pushes it to its illogical extension. If you approach the film this way, it will be a guidebook to understanding pressures your students feel.

Gregory's Girl (1981). This is a wonderful small film. It gets at the basic decency of high school students that has been my experience. It also shows how sensitive and helpful the peer group can be. The way Gregory finds out which student is interested in him is marvelous in how everyone's feelings are protected.

Dangerous Minds (1995). The characters are all two-dimensional and mostly stereotypical. The movie has little in common with LouAnne Johnson's book. But the film does have the feel for what it means for a teacher to connect with her students.

Teachers (1984). The character of Ditto alone makes the film worthwhile. Although no particular scene in the film is realistic per se, the scenes remind me of my own high school teaching experiences.

∼ Recommended Professional Education Books

Berlak, A., & Berlak, H. (1981). *Dilemmas of schooling.* New York: Methuen.

Dewey, J. (1938). *Experience and education.* New York: Macmillan.

Eisner, E. (1994). *The educational imagination* (3rd ed.). New York: Macmillan.

Eisner, E. (1991). *The enlightened eye.* New York: Macmillan.

Freire, P. (1970). *Pedagogy of the oppressed.* New York: Continuum.

Harvard Educational Review. (1968). *Socialization and schools reprint 1.* Cambridge, MA: Author.

Jackson, P. (1968). *Life in classrooms.* New York: Holt, Rinehart & Winston.

Joyce, B. (1992). *Models of teaching.* Boston: Allyn & Bacon.

Tyack, D. (1974). *The one best system.* Boston: Harvard University Press.

Tyler, R. (1950). *Basic principles of curriculum and instruction.* Chicago: University of Chicago Press.

Web Sites

Following are potentially useful Web sites. You have to browse selectively. Ideas tend to be oriented toward elementary teachers, but you can find useful ideas.

If you become interested in "leading shared inquiry," I highly recommend the training programs of the Great Books Foundation. There's probably a class already scheduled for your area, and the cost of the 2-day session is very reasonable. Contact it at http://www.greatbooks.org

I really like the concept called *4MAT*. You can see sample 4MAT lesson plans at http://www.excelcorp.com/lessons.html. This is the one commercial approach to lesson plans that truly appreciates differences and diversifies instruction.

You are always welcome to visit my eclectic Web site:
   http://www.arachnid.pepperdine.edu/goseweb/index.htm

Schrock School:
   http://www.capecod.net/schrockguide

Teachnet:
   http://www.teachnet.com

Teachers:
   http://www.teachers.net

Teachers Helping Teachers:
   http://www.pacificnet.net/.~mandel
   http://www.classroom.net

Virtual Schoolhouse:
   http://www.sunsite.unc.edu/cisco/schoolhouse

Teacher Resources on the Internet:
   http://www.oise.utoronto.ca/.~stuserv/teaching/tresourc.html

Teacher Talk:
   http://education.indiana.edu/cas/tt/tthmpg.html

Busy Teacher:
   http://www.ceismc.gatech.edu/busyt/homepg.htm

Black and African American Resources:
   http://www.clark.net/pub/briann/black.htm

References

Alshuler, A. S. (1980). *School discipline: A socially literate solution.* New York: McGraw-Hill.

Anyon, J. (1980). Social class and the hidden curriculum of work. *Journal of Education, 162*(1), 67-92.

Apple, M. W. (1977). What do schools teach? In R. H. Weller (Ed.), *Humanistic education* (pp. 27-47). Berkeley, CA: McCutchan.

Bernstein, B. (1975). *Class, codes, and control,* New York: Schocker.

Bowles, S., & Gintis, H. (1976). *Schooling in capitalist America.* New York: Basic Books.

Canter, L., & Canter, M. (1992). *Assertive discipline.* Santa Monica, CA: Lee Canter & Associates.

Chelser, M. (1966). *Role playing methods in the classroom.* Chicago: SRA.

Cohen, E. (no date). *Final report to the Center for Interracial Cooperation.* Unpublished. Contract No. OEL 9-71-0037 (508). Center for Interracial Cooperation. Principal Investigator Elizabeth G. Cohen, Stanford University.

College Board. (1983). *Academic preparation for college.* New York: Author.

Connelly, F. M. (1985). *Teachers and curriculum planners.* Toronto: Teachers College Press.

Descartes, R. (1951). *Mediations on first philosophy.* NY: MacMillan.

Dewey, J. (1938). *Experience and education.* New York: Macmillan.

Dreeben, R. (1968). *On what is learned in school.* Reading, MA: Addison-Wesley.

Eisner, E. (1979). The three curricula that all schools teach (pp. 74-92). In *The educational imagination.* New York: Macmillan.

Eisner, E. (1985). *The educational imagination.* New York: MacMillan.

Eisner, E. (1991). *The enlightened eye.* New York: Macmillan.

Ember, E. T., Evertson, C. M., Clements, B. S., Sanford, J. P., & Worsham, M. E. (1981). *Organizing and managing the junior high classroom.* Austin: University of Texas, Research and Development Center for Teacher Education.

Emerson, R. W. (1967). *Self-reliance.* Mount Vernon, NY: Peter Pauper.

Fader, D. (1976). *The new hooked on books.* New York: Berkeley Medallion.

Foster, H. (1974). *Ribbin', jivin', & playin' the dozens.* Cambridge, MA: Ballinger.

Freeman, C. (Ed.). (1996). *The wisdom of old-time baseball.* Walnut Grove, TN: Walnut Grove Press.

Freire, P. (1970). *Pedagogy of the oppressed.* New York: Continuum.

Gage, N. L., & Berliner, D. C. (1979). *Educational psychology* (2nd ed.). Chicago: Rand McNally.

Giroux, H. (1979). Social education in the classroom: The dynamics of the hidden curriculum. *Theory and Research in Social Education, 7*(1), 21-42.

Glasser, W. (1990). *Reality therapy.* New York: Harper & Row.

Gose, M. (1985, Summer). What is reality? *Kappa Delta Pi Record, 21*(4), 111-113.

Gose, M. (1986, April). A new-old pattern for classroom interaction. *Learning.*

Gose, M. (1989). Make small groups work. *California English, 25*(5), 10, 11, 19, 21.

Gray, J. (1968). *Teaching without tears.* Palo Alto, CA: Fearon.

Gray, J. (1969). *The teacher's survival guide.* Belmont, CA: Pitman.

Hart, L. (1978). The new brain concept of learning. *Phi Delta Kappan, 59*(7), 393-396.

Heller, J. (1961). *Catch 22.* NY: Simon and Schuster.

Henry, J. (1965). *Culture against man.* New York: Vintage.

Herndon, J. (1968). *The way it spozed to be.* New York: Bantam.

Herndon, J. (1971). *How to survive in your native land.* New York: Simon & Schuster.

Herndon, J. (1985). *Notes from a schoolteacher.* New York: Simon & Schuster.

Inkeles, A. (1968). The socialization of competence. *Socialization and Schools, Harvard Educational Review Reprint Number One* (pp. 65, 66).

Jackson, P. (1968). *Life in classrooms.* New York: Holt, Rinehart & Winston.

Jones, A. S., Bagford, L. W., & Wallen, E. A. (1979). *Strategies for teaching.* Metuchen, NJ: Scarecrow.

Joyce, B. (1992). *Models of teaching.* Boston: Allyn & Bacon.

Lortie, D. C. (1975). *School teacher.* Chicago: University of Chicago Press.

Orr, J. B., & Nichelson, P. F. (1970). *The radical suburb.* Philadelphia: Westminster Press.

Overly, N. (1970). *The unstudied curriculum.* Washington, DC: Association for Supervision and Curriculum Development.

Parsons, T. (1968). The school class as a social system. *Socialization and Schools, Harvard Educational Review Reprint Number One* (p. 79).

Postman, N., & Weingartner, C. (1969). *Teaching as a subversive activity*. New York: Delacorte.

Potter, S. (1931). *The theory and practice of gamesmanship*. New York: Holt, Rinehart & Winston.

Rist, R. C. (1971). Student social class and teacher expectations. *Challenging the Myths, Harvard Educational Reprint Series Number Five* (p. 107).

Sarason, S. (1982). *The culture of the school and the problem of change*. Boston: Allyn & Bacon.

Tyack, D. (1974). *The one best system*. Boston: Harvard University Press.

Tyler, R. (1950). *Basic principles of curriculum and instruction*. Chicago: University of Chicago Press.

Wittrock, W. (1985). *Handbook of research on teaching*. New York: Macmillan.

CORWIN
PRESS

The Corwin Press logo—a raven striding across an open book—represents the happy union of courage and learning. We are a professional-level publisher of books and journals for K–12 educators, and we are committed to creating and providing resources that embody these qualities. Corwin's motto is "Success for All Learners."

In compliance with GPSR, should you have any concerns about the safety of this product, please advise: International Associates Auditing & Certification Limited The Black Church, St Mary's Place, Dublin 7, D07 P4AX Ireland EUAR@ie.ia-net.com